THE FOOTBALL IMAGINA

Popular Cultural Studies

Series editors: Justin O'Connor, Steve Redhead and Derek Wynne.

The editors are, respectively, Senior Research Fellow and Co-Directors of the Manchester Institute for Popular Culture where this series is based. The Manchester Institute for Popular Culture, at The Manchester Metropolitan University, England, was set up in order to promote theoretical and empirical research in the area of contemporary popular culture, both within the academy and in conjunction with local, national and international agencies. The Institute is a postgraduate research centre engaged in comparative research projects around aspects of consumption and regulation of popular culture in the city. The Institute also runs a number of postgraduate research programmes, with a particular emphasis on ethnographic work. The series intends to reflect all aspects of the Institute's activities including its relationship with interested academics throughout the world. Current theoretical debates within the field of popular culture will be explored within an empirical context. Much of the research is undertaken by young researchers actively involved in their chosen fields of study, allowing an awareness of the issues and an attentiveness to actual developments often lacking in standard academic writings on the subject. The series will also reflect the working methods of the Institute, emphasising a collective research effort and the regular presentation of work-in-progress to the Institute's research seminars. The series hopes, therefore, both to push forward the debates around the regulation and consumption of popular culture, urban regeneration and postmodern social theory whilst introducing an ethnographic and contextual basis for such debates.

The Football Imagination

The rise of football fanzine culture

Richard Haynes

arena

Published by
Arena
Ashgate Publishing Limited
Gower House
Croft Road
Aldershot
Hants GU11 3HR
England

Ashgate Publishing Company
Old Post Road
Brookfield
Vermont 05036
USA

British Library Cataloguing in Publication Data

Haynes, Richard
    Football Imagination: Rise of Football Fanzine
    Culture. – (Popular Cultural Studies)
    I. Title   II. Series
    306.483

Library of Congress Catalog Card Number: 95-60404

ISBN 1 85742 212 0 (Hardback)
ISBN 1 85742 213 9 (Paperback)

Printed and bound in Great Britain by
Hartnolls Limited, Bodmin, Cornwall

Contents

Author's note:

*This is an updated version of Chapter 4 in S. Redhead, (ed.), 1993, *The Passion and the Fashion*, Avebury, Aldershot.

**This is a completely rewritten version of Chapter 5 in S. Redhead, (ed.), 1993, *The Passion and the Fashion*, Avebury, Aldershot.

Acknowledgements

Special thanks to Steve Redhead, Alan Haughton, Nikos Michas, Antonio Melechi, Hillegonda Rietveld, Adam Brown, Mick Day, Rocco De Biasi, Derek Wynne, Justin O'Connor, David Jary, Andy Lyons, Bill Brewster, Guy Lovelady, Pete Naylor, Ian Taylor, Vic Duke, Andy Ward, Jim Cooke, Dave Sewell, Colin Beveridge, Nick Wheat, Speed, Jane Purdon, John Tummon, Alex Griffiths, Dylan Jones, Linda Whitehead, Janet Bailey, David Outram, Steve Sadler, Alfie O'Docherty, Dan Devine, Ian Standish, Paul Clarke, Maggy Taylor, Janet and Bill Lievers, Anthony and Jackie Haynes, and Susan Spinelli.

Preface

The Football Imagination presents a narrative about the mushrooming of football fanzine subculture within an emerging, interdisciplinary Popular Cultural Studies. Entry into the football fan subculture as an ethnographer was premised upon my previous knowledge and experience of football - as both amateur player and supporter - reflecting the symbiotic relationship I and many other mates of my generation (I was born in the sixties and grew up to love the game in the seventies) have with the previous generations and cultural traditions of football in British society. Hence, the book not only rested on my powers of observation as an ethnographer, but is inherently self-reflective. My biography was also crucial as it became apparent before conducting the research that many of those involved in the production, distribution and consumption of football fanzines were, *prima facie*, of my generation, sex, ethnic origin, and educational background. Moreover, the similarities transcend the football domain into a whole series of leisure and cultural practices: from popular music, fashion, television, drinking and clubbing, to name but a few. Finally, and most importantly regarding the motivation for undertaking the research, was the opinion that supporters have a productive role within the football industry, specifically given the elevation of the sport on the political agenda in the dark shadow cast by the tragic events at Heysel, Bradford and Hillsborough. Both theoretically and empirically the study of football fanzines runs contrary to the belief that spectators are irrelevant to the success of the game, or (as in the preoccupation with 'hooliganism') the pathological viewpoint which sees fans as dangerous, portrayed through images of deviance.

The major empirical project involved the accumulation of a fanzine archive, providing a rich source of written data, and performing as a contemporary oral history of football fandom. The fanzines were collated over a period of two years, building on a preexisting archive set up by Steve Redhead. There were several methods of obtaining fanzines: by post, systematically approaching the editors of titles which appeared in the lists of *When Saturday Comes* or *The Absolute Game*; via the numerous points of distribution - outside grounds on match days, independent record stores and sports book/programme shops; and finally, donations from family, friends and colleagues. The description of the archive, its archaeology, was an important methodology in tracing the genealogy of fanzines and football discourse, enabling the analysis of transformations in the fanzine subculture and texts in their specificity. This historical analysis involved both a textual reading of fanzines and biographical detail of their contributors, obtained through letters, interviews and informal conversations (see, for instance, the history of *WSC.*). During many of the interviews, which were open-ended and semi-structured, the fanzine writer or editor had prior knowledge of the research project. However, a large proportion of the book draws upon conventional participant observation of supporters and fanzine contributors and sellers, where my identity as an academic researcher was not disclosed. For instance, I would attend FSA. meetings in Manchester, where editors were frequently present and would exploit these contacts to obtain valuable anecdotes on either the production of the fanzines or, invariably, the latest political wranglings of the editors beloved club. My strategy was completely flexible, often relying on, impromptu meetings. Where possible interviews were tape recorded, but, more often than not, I relied upon powers of memory as I wrote up notes of my various conversations and experiences.

The geographical location of the research is of consequence, in both the archiving of fanzines and the flow of information available. Although the archive set out to collect at least one copy of every fanzine title produced - in the UK and Europe - the availability of fanzines produced in the North West and individuals in the area willing to donate their own collections did provide a more than adequate representation of publications in the North West. Similarly, I was far more likely to get involved in (or overhear) conversations regarding clubs in the North West than those in London and, as I have insisted throughout the book, the oral tradition of football, usually carried on in the pub, is a significant part of football's discursive field. Therefore, what is said about football in a pub in Manchester is likely to be different to what is said about the game in London. These nuances in football discourse are part of the 'indefinitely describable field of relationships' (Foucault, 1991) at any given time. The case study of Leeds United fans is due to my own biography of supporting the club and the numerous friends and contacts developed over several years of living and working in the city.

The major problem of conducting the research and in writing the book was the sheer size of the fanzine phenomenon. The ephemeral nature of fanzines denies the archivist a realistic opportunity to obtain the myriad tithes produced since the mid 80s. Furthermore, given the number of fanzines I eventually collected, it became impossible to read all of them (even if desired) and so my textual search for material concentrated around specific themes, i.e. ID. cards, policing, the 'super league', racism, and other political articles associated to individual clubs. Having said this, I always kept an eye out for the unusual, the humorous and the contentious. Finally, in writing the book I was always conscious of the two, yet not mutually exclusive audiences: football fans and academic critics of sport. My love of football would often conflict with my intellectual scrutiny of the sport. However, the intelligence and innovative spirit of what Adrian Goldberg termed the 'Radical Football Faction', which includes not only fanzines, but independent supporters groups and the general 'carnivalesque' feeling of football fandom in the nineties did more than appease my worries that I was studying the world's number one sport.

About the author

Richard Haynes is co-author of *The Passion and the Fashion: Football Fandom in the New Europe,* edited by S. Redhead (Avebury, 1993).   Between 1990-92 he was a Research Assistant at the Manchester Institute for Popular Culture at The Manchester Metropolitan University. He is currently funded by the ESRC to research the future of the televised football industry at the John Logie Baird Centre at the Universities of Strathclyde and Glasgow, in conjunction with the Department of Film and Media Studies, University of Stirling.

Introduction

The failure of England's national side to reach the finals of the 1994 World Cup Finals in the USA has once again put into sharp focus the crisis of the 'national' game. This navel gazing is made all the more acute given the prospect of the European Nation's Championship to be held in England in 1996, thirty years on from the last time a major football tournament was held in the country which regards itself as the 'home' of football. The immediate debate has concentrated on the structure of the game, specifically its management and coaching strategies - a discourse which has been prevalent in the English game since the national side was humbled by Hungary and Puskas in 1953. However, the locus of this debate is more than likely to shift towards the behaviour of the English supporters, both domestically and internationally. While the panoptic gaze on football supporters is nothing new, knowledge of an alternative football culture has entered the national consciousness, invariably drawing attention to the victimisation of football fans. Football fans have been integral to recent changes in football culture. *Fever Pitch* (Gollancz, 1992), Nick Hornby's biographical treatise of growing up and being a football fan is heavily influenced by a new breed of football writing which has emerged from fanzines, and the book's critical acclaim (Sports book of the Year, 1992 and short listing for the 1993 NCR award) signifies a widening, in terms of cultural taste, of football's audience.

1 A novel school of thought: Football theory into fanzine theory

It cannot go unnoticed to any new scholar in the field of football culture, that the overwhelming point of enquiry into 'the peoples game' is that of 'football hooliganism'. From Ian Taylor's speculations on the nature of 'soccer consciousness' and 'soccer hooliganism' in the late 60s to the sociological and historical project undertaken by Eric Dunning and his colleagues into the *Roots of Football Hooliganism* throughout the 80s, the study of football invariably manifests itself into an account of violence in and around football. It is almost as if the contemporary history of English soccer is that of the 'football hooligan'. No doubt many Members of Parliament in the present government and those of the 1980s with a penchant for 'law and order' would adhere to such a view. So too would the 'free marketeers' eager to make a 'quick buck', turn football into a sterile media spectacle or better still, be have done with the game to make way for the more genteel pleasures of shopping, within a highly modern, high security shopping centre where the attendance of the family is assured on a Saturday afternoon. As Duke (1991) has argued, the lack of consideration to other aspects of the game and its support may be symptomatic of the "high visibility in media discourse" of the 'hooligan problem' which in turn gives merit to funding for "policy related research". The wealth, in numbers and not necessarily in content, of literature on football related violence has become a veritable industry. This was recognized as such by Ian Taylor as far back as 1972, who in a review of Hunter Davies' book *The Glory Game* stated:

3

Nowadays, it's not only the so-called hooligans who look for diversion and excitement in the glorification of professional soccer. It's also the middlebrow, button-down-collar 'intellectuals' of the Sunday press, and academics from various disciplines who can now write their football hang-ups without loss of respectability (*New Society* 26.10.72).

Twenty years on and football is gaining a new respectability, this time from the fans themselves who now enthuse about the glory of the game on the pages of fanzines. This momentous turn in the way the game is written and thought about has forced a recognition among academics for a broader approach to football research. As we enter the final decade of the century a new mood, or to use Raymond Williams' (1961) term 'structure of feeling', has permeated the game, where fans are more willing and capable of expressing their opinions to an industry that faces many problems, not least that of modernity. Duke (1991) outlines what he sees as a set of seven 'positive indicators' within English football: increased attendances; decreased violence inside the stadium; expanded volume of football literature; heightened interest as a result of the World Cup finals; return to European club competitions; extended sponsorship of football; growing competition for television coverage. While some of these indicators could be argued to carry some negative connotations for the game, not least the increasing penetration of satellite television into the way the game is organized, the general feeling among many academics and supporters alike is far more optimistic than could be thought fifteen, even ten years ago. This is attested by the publication of books like Lansdown and Spillius (1990), Redhead (1991), Williams and Wagg (1991), Cosgrove (1991) a whole edition of *The Sociological Review* (Vol. 39 No. 3) and the popularity of fanzines such as *When Saturday Comes* and *The Absolute Game*. All of these publications carry or are imbued with a far more sanguine view of football in the 1990s.

The title of this chapter is taken from a fanzine produced in London, epitomizing many of the general fanzines available throughout Britain and Europe. It is towards a novel school of thought about researching and writing about the game that this chapter is centred. Through the study of fanzines the whole book attempts to discover, as Redhead (1991a, p.11) puts it "why football as popular culture is a source of such multiple pleasures for its millions of fans". Such a task

4

is complicated by the aforementioned bias in the study of football fan culture of the past twenty years. However, as I have also highlighted, recent analysis has attempted to shed the shackles of researching 'hooliganism' (so reminiscent of the containment of fans themselves) and sought several different paths of enquiry. However, the 'football hooligan' discourse cannot be ignored, as its two main groups of scholars: Ian Taylor and other Marxist scholars; and Eric Dunning and his colleagues at Leicester University, have helped to establish football as a realm worthy of sociological study and research. Moreover, both 'schools of thought', which are far from homogeneous in their nature, are of indirect significance to the study of fanzines. What follows is a description and critique of Taylor's and Dunning et al's work on football. Far from presenting a caricature of their work the analysis attempts to highlight aspects of their research most pertinent to the study of fanzines.

The work of Ian Taylor

Serious sociological analysis of football is commonly recognized to have begun with Ian Taylor's "Soccer Consciousness and Soccer hooliganism" which appeared in *Images of Deviance* edited by Stan Cohen (1971). The book consisted of a collection of papers given at the York Deviancy Symposium where the range of subjects studied varied from marijuana smoking, industrial sabotage, and the functions of coroners to football hooliganism. This brand of sociology was interested in the mass media's role in the construction of social and political consensus. 'Football hooliganism' had become an explicit public concern in the late 1960s, in part determined by definitions of the normal, the acceptable and the deviant as played out in the media.

Although the early work of Taylor on football has been criticized for its lack of empirical data and its "romanticised view of the past" (Dunning et al 1988, Young 1991) it does nonetheless pose some interesting questions about supporters' links with a club and the wider affect of society on the game itself. The idea of 'soccer consciousness' refers to the social and psychological meanings of the English football fan. Football for many working class boys is the dominant sport in their lives. Taylor couples the values of soccer (masculinity, victory, and group participation) with the historical experience of the English working class. Leaving arguments about the origins of 'hooliganism' aside, implicit in Taylor's thesis is the belief in a specific relationship between fans, the historical development of the game and English working class experience. A concept of 'participatory democracy' is introduced, evoking a perceived relationship between the fans and the club they supported, whereby the fans exerted an influence on club policy and "the welfare of the team" (1971, p.143). However, this 'participatory democracy' declined in the late 1950s due to 'bourgeoisification' of the game due to the conjuncture between an emerging affluent society and changing leisure relations, represented by football authorities' attempts to attract a more 'middle class' spectatorship. As Taylor puts it:

> Soccer has become professionalised in a very special sense, and the idea of the 'true' soccer supporter has been transformed - at least in the eyes of soccer's powerful and the mass media at large (1971, p.143).

Furthermore, a process of 'internationalization', as Taylor termed it, caused fractures in the relationship between the fans and the club, as styles of play became increasingly more professionalized to compete in international competition, intended to add colour to soccer within an emerging 'society of leisure'. Ultimately, this led to a form of soccer where:

> ... the clubs are increasingly concerned to provide a passive form of spectacle, and a soccer that is dominated by financial rather than by sub-cultural relationships (1971, p.150).

The changes in the game led to the assertion by some members of the working class of an inarticulate societal reaction; resistance through violence. Taylor believes that such violence around football was an attempt to express a "Keenly experienced sense of control over 'the game that was theirs' ".

The early work of Taylor was no more than a speculative attempt to introduce a sociological account of the changes occurring within the game. However, the processes of change, that he was attempting to explain have some relevance to the contemporary football milieu - even when no direct comparisons can be made. The contemporary voice of the fanzines and the Football Supporters Association to 'reclaim the game' are imbued with a similar nostalgia for a past form of democracy within football, whether real or imagined. The social and political reaction of contemporary fans to 'commercialization', 'globalization' and 'modernization' compares favourably with the processes Taylor was trying to theorize. Yet, the major difference between what Taylor saw as a 'resistance movement' to such processes and what today could be termed a 'culture of defence' by fans, is that the former manifested itself in violence, while the latter is a form of opposition to violence, and to the labelling of all fans as 'hooligans'.

We turn now to the later work of Taylor, which can be characterized as post-Heysel, dealing with what he calls a "fundamental crisis" of professional football in Britain. Indeed, Taylor characterizes the disastrous events at Bradford and Heysel as representing an "exceptional moment" in the history of British football subsequently followed by the tragedy at Hillsborough, which had a subsequent influence on the work of Taylor, a life long supporter of Sheffield Wednesday.

The review of Taylor's later work is drawn from four articles from the mid 80s to the early 90s: reflections after Bradford and Brussels (Taylor 1987), his "personal contemplations" after Hillsborough (Taylor 1989), a paper given to a colloquium on 'Football and Europe' at the European University Institute (Taylor 1990) and an updated and revised edition of the Hillsborough article (Taylor 1991). All four, to a certain degree share common concerns: political economy of football in English society; official and popular discourse on disasters at football; modernization of football in the new Europe; and the cultural politics of football spectatorship.

Taylor's political economy of football in English society is centred around the tragic events at Bradford, Heysel and Hillsborough. The latter two events are considered to have certain ideological, "discursive connections", based around a theme of disasters, the Thatcher years being littered with a series of disasters, inner city riots, and breakdowns in 'efficacy' of public provisions. The model of a competitive free market in Britain offers no guarantee of safety or adequate public provision. Football's crisis was compounded by the rhetoric of the New Right in the early to mid 80s, the Thatcher Government mounting an ideological attack on football on the grounds of 'law and orderism'. Following similar analysis by

Seabrook (1978) and Hall and Jacques (1983) Taylor argues that this new 'State Capitalism' arose due to the "underextension of post-war social democracy" (1987, p.176), and encapsulated a "hidden agenda" against football. This retrenchment and attack against football was due to a perceived 'disappearance' of class, the introduction of market-orientated modernization, and the belief that soccer was a "slum sport for slum people" (1987, p.182). However, Taylor insists that a critique of the radical Right must be accompanied with a realization of soccer's *real* crisis during the 1980s. It is for this reason he argues:

> ... it must be recognised that the right wing's *description* of soccer's present unhappy condition *is* much more true to the actual popular experience of soccer than are the more sanguine accounts proffered by soccer's own administrators or its apologists among television commentators (1987, p.183).

Moreover, Taylor argues that the game's style and presentation compounds the lack of sympathy for soccer in this country due to its "disciplined" and "unpoetic" nature. But Taylor still contends that football continues to reach aspects of the 'social' being as opposed to fulfilment in private life or in ritualized public consumerism. Throughout his work, it is argued that public life and public provision are important in and of themselves. The future of soccer lies in the recognition and challenge of broader class inequalities, looking towards economic and social needs of people, that is, soccer as a 'social provision' with local and national investment. Taylor also urges soccer administrators to make political decisions against the mythologies of the market. Ultimately, Hillsborough represented:

> The end-point of a period of experiment in which, as the Prime Minister herself once insistently suggested, there is no such thing as the social (1989, p.110).

Taylor's critique of the radical Right's economic and political agenda for football in conjunction with his thoughts of a socialist's future for football are incorporated within the second characteristic of his work relating to 'official' and 'popular' discourses on football disasters. The critique of 'official discourse', a term taken from Burton and Carlen (1979), highlights the fact that all enquiries in this country with regard to disasters such as Bradford, Heysel and Hillsborough, are conducted by the judiciary, a function of their "refined understanding and practice" (1989, p.99). Yet, the Popplewell report (1986) represented an example of "over determination" of crowd safety issues by those of law and order, proposing the extension of police powers. By lumping the events of Bradford and Heysel together the Report poorly interprets the "differing order of significance" of "quite different interpretations of the crisis of British soccer" (1987, p.172). The Report's findings are then, contends Taylor, symptomatic of the broader political climate and the rhetoric of the radical Right regarding football. Similar fears were held by Taylor in the aftermath of the Hillsborough tragedy with regard to the enquiry by Lord Justice Taylor. However, these reservations were laid to rest with the publication of Lord Justice Taylor's Final Report, which came out favourably for football: arguing for the removal of perimeter fences; rejecting the Government's ID card scheme; and denouncing the squalid facilities at football grounds. The Report demanded radical modernization and Taylor argued that the inquest was important in the 'symbolic realm'. It is here that the 'popular discourse' of football, and the events at Hillsborough particularly, play a crucial role in the analysis. The continuation of normal relations between club and community, a process Taylor had analysed in the early seventies, was rendered problematic in the aftermath of Hillsborough. As argued before, football had lost contact with its 'traditional constituency', the notion of 'participatory democracy' and the 'people's game' as envisaged by Arthur Hopcraft. It was after Hillsborough that there occurred a 'reconstruction' of these bonds, emphasizing the role of the football ground as 'shrine'. The decorations outside Hillsborough and on the terraces at Anfield symbolized a "mass popular religious rite" which marked a "cleansing" of the game (1989, p.91). It is argued that after Heysel it was difficult to see how football could once again mobilize popular support. But with a successful World Cup campaign by England in 1990 and the emergence of fanzines and the FSA, there appears to be a noticeable change in mood. However, Taylor is weary of the cynical opposition towards aspects of the Taylor Report emanating from fanzines and the FSA, specifically over the issue of all-seater stadiums, where supporters refer to "architectural determinism". Taylor believes the supporters lobby has misunderstood the "overall strategic agenda" of the Report, the fans'

9

opposition being built on "inert, reactionary, nostalgia" reminiscent of the football authorities' own refusal to modernize over the years. The defence of "terrace culture" is deemed a "fantastic" representation of "actual terrace culture" as it is experienced (1991, p.14).

It is the political and economic climate of the 80s and early 90s allied with legal and popular debates on football that Taylor moves his analysis on with questions about "modernisation" and "Europeanization". The new sense of reform and change being experienced by football at the present conjuncture is a result of what Taylor termed the "crisis of English soccer". Stadiums are in dire need of modernization, the Bradford fire is cited as a prime example of what can happen if this process is not undertaken. Taylor refers to the "decaying of Liverpool" as a symbol of decline and lack of interest in modernization within British towns and cities. He emphasizes that modernization is a 'social process' and that the tragedy of Hillsborough arose because of a countering social process of containment, stemming from the late 1960s. The Leppings Lane end was continually reconstructed as a caged-in pen. Although the *Taylor Report* was quick to dismiss the rhetoric of 'law and order' it is argued that it fails to address "economic and cultural contingencies which may obstruct or enable the new project of modernisation" (1991, p.17). The fundamental problem has been capital investment in post-war years, and the limitations of "free market individualism". Taylor is looking forward to a new "common European home", with rapid liberalization in a pluralist, post-industrial society: a soccer *perestroika* (1990, p.6). Popular sports, specifically football, are considered to have the possibilities of opening up a dialogue between ordinary citizens of the EC.

Taylor's most apposite work with regard to fanzines is that on the culture of football supporters in Britain. As cited before his early speculations on football culture were symptomatic of the media's concern over 'football hooliganism'. The issue of hooliganism is continued in the analysis of the major disasters of the 80s. It is pointed out that the Hillsborough disaster was seen by many across Europe as an expression of English hooliganism, tribal aggression that has grown up over the last two decades of English football, resiliently masculinist and chauvinistic. Taylor sets about explaining why such a view could arise out of a tragedy that had more to do with attempts to curb 'hooliganism' and not out of actual acts of violence. This theoretical argument also enables a mapping out of distinct cultural aspects of violent football support from the mid 60s to the dislocation of working class people from the mid 60s, due largely to industrial modernization, growth in affluence, the emergence of youth culture and processes of rehousing. The revolution of rising expectations manifested itself in consumerism, structural developments within the class, and embourgeoisement. The new bourgeois workers' cultural preoccupations were generated by dominant institutions and also reflected the dislocation of individuals' insecure class position. In the event, this led to many working class football fans being drawn to the racist politics of the National Front, which became deeply associated with football in the late 70s.

Taylor characterizes the last three decades of football violence as having three shifts underlying its manifestation. Violence from the mid to late 60s was a reaction on the part of the traditional working class to changes in social organization of the game. Violence from the mid to late 70s was an expression of economic anxieties of working class youth which manifested itself as ritual aggression against an 'imagined enemy'. Finally, violence in the 80s occurred within a different conjuncture, where generalized anxieties affect both bourgeois and traditional workers but differently. The absence of a social democratic political/economic programme led to a "more intense nihilistic form of racist, sexist and nationalist paranoia", reminiscent to what Taylor describes as "barbarism" (1987, p.179). However, hooliganism is seen as a product of culture not simply a product of social deprivation. Much violence around football is considered to be based on a "residual sense of solidarity" and Raymond Williams' idea of 'mobile privatization' is used to explain the neighbourhood ties of gender and race which foregrounds much jingoistic nationalism among fans. The overriding 'conditions of experience' of fans involved in violence is one of moral and cultural shallowness, due to a general lack of alternative experience.

The fracturing of the working class along with the racism and tribalism of the terraces made the defence of soccer difficult in the 80s, the game increasingly finding itself incapable of mobilizing support due to the way it presented itself. However, Taylor argues that a 'new future' is in sight resulting from the crisis soccer experienced during the 80s. There is a 'real sense' of the contribution a "revitalised and exciting" game could make to national and local culture. Taylor has cited the 'carnivalesque' nature of West Ham fans during their team's defeat by Nottingham Forest in the 1991 FA Cup semi-final as an instance of a revitalized fan culture (*Independent on Sunday*, 21.4.91).

Finally, in his paper to the international conference on football at the European University Institute, Florence, Taylor asked if it is sensible to identity football as the 'object of analysis' at all? By this he was referring to the way in which football discourse swings wildly from the game itself to news or gossip about personalities to political economy or law and order. A central theoretical theme should be a recognition of the existence of the discourse that is 'talk about football': namely *male talk*, a form of working class 'common sense'. Talking about football exerts a hegemonic influence on gender relations, epitomized by the 'working class weekend'. Football interest has been constructed anew as a response to the recent crisis, yet remains local, conservative and male. What Taylor argues for is a "knowing and reflexive leadership of football" that would recognize many of the issues concerning football are *not* really football's issues in any simple sense.

The Leicester school of thought

Approached by academics, students, journalists, football clubs, supporters, police forces, politicians, local authorities, Ministers for Sport and government departments, the Sir Norman Chester Centre for Football Research has achieved no mean feat in establishing itself as the preeminent producer of research, statistics and information on soccer. Set up in 1987 and named after its first patron Sir Norman Chester, who was Deputy Chairman of the Football Trust and author of two government reports on the state of English football in 1968 and 1983, the Leicester school of thought, as I shall refer to it, has in one form or another been conducting research on football for more than twenty years. Eric Dunning has been the prime mover of the research centre inspired by the work of a German born academic, Norbert Elias. Concentrated research on the behaviour of football spectators began in 1979, firstly with a grant from the then Social Science Research Council and latterly with funds from the Football Trust. The Leicester scholars have produced a number of reports, articles and books, which includes the annual *Digest of Football*

Statistics for the Football Trust. They have amassed the largest amount of empirical data on football in Britain, if not Europe, and their theoretical framework for the study of 'hooliganism' has influenced the study of violence in sport both in Europe and America (see Young, 1991). My critique of their work will commence with an overview of their project to discover the sociological and historical roots of 'football hooliganism', followed by an outline of possible applications of their work to the study of fanzines, and finally an expose of tensions and constraints that their theoretical framework poses for the study of football as popular culture.

In his recent articles and speeches on football, Eric Dunning and his colleagues Patrick Murphy and Ivan Waddington have been quick to reassert their faith in 'figurational sociology' or 'process sociological' approaches to studying sport and particularly sports related violence (Dunning et al 1991, p.1992). The defence of their methods hot on the heels of recent critiques, namely those of Armstrong and Harris (1991) and Clarke (1991), has occurred at an interesting juncture in the history of research undertaken by the Leicester team. Interestingly, the research of John Williams and Rogan Taylor appears to be aimed towards a new set of goal posts. By this it is meant that within their own terms Williams and Taylor have set out to investigate other aspects of the whole football figuration as opposed to exclusively issues concerning 'hooliganism', aspects which do not readily adhere to the theoretical stringencies traditionally associated with the Leicester school. Moreover, where Williams' work still involves research into hooliganism, it is written with terminology usually associated with cultural studies as developed out of Marxism, semiotics and discourse theory, without mention of figurations. This is not to suggest that Williams has discarded or reneged previous research undertaken by himself and other members of the Leicester school, but merely to recognize that a noticeable change and shift in emphasis in his work has occurred. This is a matter to return to later, but first an account of the work which is traditionally associated with Leicester and which has received considerable attention by a variety of agencies involved in the game.

Given the immense amount of literature that has flowed from the Centre it would be impossible to do justice to the various projects undertaken by Dunning and his colleagues in a summary such as this. Therefore, what follows is based on their major sociological and historical project: the roots of football hooliganism. Space shall be given later to the more recent and invigorating work which has covered issues of modernization, gender, racism and other issues within the game which are analysed outside the orbit of figurational sociology. In view of Dunning et al's (1991) retort against recent criticism the review of their work will attempt to avoid the protagonistic pitfalls of misconstructing and parodying their research, to achieve a fair reflection of the Leicester School.

The first stage in their research into 'football hooliganism' rested on the work of John Williams as a participant observer in three case studies: the 1982 World Cup in Spain; the 1982 European Cup Final in Rotterdam; and a European Championship game between England and Denmark in Copenhagen during the same year. Williams was considered to be "young enough and sufficiently 'street wise' and interested in football to pass himself off as an 'ordinary' English football fan" (1989, preface to second edition). His findings, coupled with a theoretical input from Dunning and Murphy, were published in *Hooligans Abroad* (1984). The second book, and main body of work, *The Roots of Football Hooliganism* (1988) is an historical study which traces variations in the reported incidence of soccer crowd disorderliness and football hooliganism from the beginnings of the professional game in the 1870s and 1880s to the present day. Their third book in the Routledge series, *Football On Trial* (1990), is an assortment of essays on a similar theme with the addition of an ethnography of 'lads' from a Leicester council estate researched in the early 80s and a couple of articles looking towards the future of the game. All three books, while employing a variety of research methods, have a theoretical underpinning of the 'civilizing process' as developed by Elias and 'ordered segmentation' as developed by Suttles.

An extensive account of the application of Eliandian Theory to the study of 'football hooliganism' is given in *The Figurational Approach to Leisure and Sport* (Dunning 1989) and a defence of the empirical research is given in Dunning, Murphy and Waddington's contribution to *The Sociological Review* (Vol. 39 No. 3). Both suppositions offer concise arguments for a figurational sociology of sport. In short, Dunning observes that no decade in the history of the game has passed without instances of violence on a substantial scale. When plotted historically, incidence occurs in a U-shaped curve: high before the First World War, dropping between the wars and remaining relatively low until the mid 50s, and finally, escalating again in the mid 60s. Early violence is distinguished as occurring against players and referees in contrast to the later violence between groups of fans. This historical pattern is set against the theoretical background of the 'civilizing process'. Following Elias, Dunning argues:

> ... in Western European societies since the Middle Ages, a more or less continuous elaboration and refinement of manners and social standards can be shown to have taken place (1989, p.42).

In relation to football, this infers a long term decline in people's propensity for obtaining pleasure from directly engaging in or witnessing violent acts in and around football. The majority of 'hard core hooligans' are considered to have emerged from the socioeconomically worst off section of the working class, who have not been subjected to 'civilizing processes' anything like as much as those further up the social hierarchy. Trapped in relative poverty they are more prone to violent behaviour. In this respect Dunning concludes:

> The fact that members of the 'rougher' sections of the working class grew up in a situation of severely limited power chances, live with a level of violence in excess of that which is usually experienced by groups higher up the scale and that many of them experience rough treatment at the hands of the police, has manifold consequences for their personality, their social standards and the structure of the communities that they form (1989, p.49).

Suttle's concept of 'ordered segmentation' is referred to as a 'hypothetical explanation' of the sociogenisis of football gangs (crews) and to complement arguments about "aggressive masculinity". Empirical data based on participant observation and interviews from Leicester's West Kingsley and Old Garden estates in 1980/81 are used to substantiate the theory that inter-estate conflicts are obsequious once the lads are on the Filbert Street terraces of Leicester City, united in opposition to visiting fans. And so it goes for regional, national and international confrontations. Finally, in the Leicester School's defence of the figurational approach that they have adhered to unabatedly throughout their work on 'football

15

hooliganism' it is argued that a catholic view of method has been employed to avoid one-dimensionalism, thus penetrating the phenomenon empirically and theoretically.

It is probably the fastidious quest for empirical data, for instance the historical work on the *Leicester Mercury* or the compilation of the *Digest of Football Statistics*, that has led certain members of the school to reconsider the theoretical merits of the figurational approach to the study of the game. Much of the qualitative data collected by Williams has not appeared or has been channelled into the theoretical stringencies that the Leicester research is geared towards. It is the admission of such a fact that Williams has written several articles and given numerous conference papers that fall outside the remit of Eliandian theory. Moreover, the introduction of Rogan Taylor, founder of the FSA, and a large number of researchers in the SNCCFR, has forced a broadening of Leicester's research agenda. Burning issues of democratization and modernization within football have led to a series of small research projects on women, ethnic football cultures, fanzines, and the FSA. Numerous reports have therefore appeared from the Centre dealing with the above issues, chiefly in a policy orientated manner. In a sense, the policy orientated bent of the Centre was envisaged as the next step in the research process after the initial study into *The Roots of Football Hooliganism*. The Centre is perceived as a 'think tank' on football, its recommendations are highly regarded in policy making circles (see for example Lord Justice Taylor's Interim Report).

Critics of the Leicester School, most notably Clarke (1991), have suggested that the use of Eliandian theory allied with the policy orientated approach, has had its own 'civilizing' effect on its disciples, which in turn, has created a hegemonic position in the field of football research. Ironically, the focus on studying discourses of containment - segregation, separation, and surveillance - creates a space for legal discourses to operate, allowing the mechanisms of control to apply Leicester's taxonomy of football fan behaviour. Clarke (1991, p.5) argues that Leicester's analysis, on their own terms, "focuses on a sub-category of the figuration being studied" which presents "an account of a marginal minority within the figuration". The lack of sociological knowledge on why people become football fans, within particular patterns of support, leads Clarke to suggest:

An ethnography of the fans which unpacked the scale of meaning given to them by their experience within the context outlined by the political economy of leisure is necessary if we are to make a break through in explaining behaviour patterns (Clarke,1991, p.26).

The ethnographic vigour of Leicester's work has been called into question by the recent studies of Gary Armstrong (with Harris 1991, and 1992) and Richard Giulianotti (1991b). Drawing from his ethnography of Sheffield United fans (the Blades), investigating 'hooliganism' from the social actors' viewpoint, Armstrong contends that Leicester's data provides only 'apt illustrations' for their theoretical understanding of the macro-social structure. Challenging the use of statistics as 'facts', Armstrong shows contempt for the insufficient nature of grand theory to examine the level and frequency of violence at football. The following description of his findings stands in stark contrast to the general impression portrayed in the work of Dunning et al, and also Ian Taylor's theory of a crisis in the 'capitalist hegemony' of Britain:

The Blades were in no way influenced by outside Fascist groups, had no 'General' or hierarchical structure and unlike some sociologists could differentiate amongst their ranks and could speak of 'rough' lads both in a football and non-football context. The composition of the 'core' hooligans were not the lower working class of Sheffield. The level of violence was also far lower than observers would have us believe. Blades realized the diversity of their members even if the media and police and researchers lump them together and label them (Armstrong, 1992, p.25).

However, despite the richness of Armstrong's work it can be argued that 'hooligan' ethnographies have reached, in the words of Redhead (1991b;481), a "limit of effectiveness in terms of explanatory power". This is, in part, due to the production of media images of 'football hooliganism' resulting in the signification between football and violence. It would, therefore, seem more appropriate to apply recent notions of 'hyperreality' where images of reality precede the event. In a sophisticated synthesis of ethnography and poststructuralist (postmodernist) studies on football, Giulianotti, through his

17

understanding of Scottish football 'casual' and youth culture, has significantly updated studies, not only on 'hooliganism', but British football culture as a whole. With an illuminating combination of participant observation and critical theory, Giulianotti uncovers the Scottish fan habitus (with the media persona of the Tartan Army), highlighting the capacity of fans, as individuals and social formations, to recognize powers of agency, enabling and empowering themselves to oppose or subvert dominant discourses of British football fans. This transcendence of 'hooligan discourses' is vital with regard to the study of football fanzine culture and independent supporters organizations.

Attempts to transcend the Eliandian focus of sociological studies on football have also appeared within other European countries. In Italy, the study of the 'Ultras' (fanatical supporters) has prompted both the use of Dunning et al's approach by Roversi and alternative theories which deny the applicability of 'figurational sociology' to the Italian context, most notably by Del Lago and De Biassi from Milan. Work by Bromberger (1993a and 1993b) on French and Italian football is symptomatic of a broader approach being adopted within football research. These studies have opened up our understanding of football fandom, by asking questions about the game's universal appeal, its masculine rituals (not necessarily related to violence), the symbolic investments of fans when supporting their team, and the carnivalesque nature of football fandom. While not to deny the continuing occurrence of violent behaviour in relation to the sport (and indeed other sports), researchers in England have been forced to acknowledge a noticeable shift in the prevailing domestic club football.

This urge to carnival is most strikingly illustrated by the mushrooming of football fanzines. Prior to this research, only a token acknowledgement of the importance of fanzines had appeared within sociological research on football: Bucke's (1988) exploratory survey of fanzines for the Sir Norman Chester Centre; Jary and Horne's (1990) paper on fanzines and contestation within popular culture drawing on theories of sport and hegemony which was later updated with Bucke's data and published in *The Sociological Review* a year later (Jary, Horne and Bucke, 1991); and Steve Redhead's (1987) pastiche of pop culture writing in *Sing When You're Winning* which focused on football as a popular cultural product at a time when fanzines were produced by a mere handful of enthusiasts with no conception of what they had started. Several journalistic and scrapbook treatise to football fanzines were also published, most notably Shaw (1989), Lacey (1989) and Robinson (1989). All of the above pay homage to the punk ancestry of fanzines, which basically lies in a DIY ethos, and also to the forerunner of football's contemporary alternative press *Foul*, which was published between 1972-76.

Taking an eclectic, qualitative approach, this research takes its shape around a unique fanzine archive within the Manchester Institute for Popular Culture (originally conceived in the Unit for Law and Popular Culture), at The Manchester Metropolitan University, which was already of a considerable size and substance, thanks to the initial work of my colleagues Alan Haughton and Steve Redhead. The archive was established not only out of a posterity, to capture the fleeting success (and excess) of a popular cultural form, but also as a rich resource of textual data that could be used as a form of oral history on football. The maintenance and renewal of the archive had the unforgiving objective of collecting at least one copy of every sports related fanzine ever produced. I say this for the simple reason that fanzines can often come and go with alarming alacrity. Yet, it is this ephemerality which characterizes the whole phenomenon: the elusiveness of fanzines ends up being their seductiveness for the die-hard collector. Therefore, it was no surprise to me, after two years of research and collecting fanzines, to estimate the number of titles, which have appeared and disappeared, as approaching 1000. Many of these titles have changed name and are edited by the same people, many more arise to fill a perceived gap in the market, whether or not a club already has a fanzine dedicated to it. It is not uncommon for one club to have three, four, even five fanzines independently dedicated to them, each carving out its own niche, taking in their own subtle brand of humour and skit criticism.

2 Waiting for the great leap forward (1): The genealogy of football writing

The emergence of fanzines as a new 'Radical Football Faction', as Adrian Goldberg coined it in the first issue of *Off The Ball*, has a genealogy that can be traced through various popular culture discourses: from a history of football journalism and literature to the vitriolic pen of a new (postmodern) football writing style; from the underground press of the 60s and DIY ethos of punk and assorted music fanzines to the ironic subversion of Thatcherite 'enterprise culture' by the soccer casual and producers of football fanzines. Various strands of popular culture - literature, music, fashion and football - thread together to form the current 'soccer consciousness' (Taylor, 1971) and imagination, which have been meticulously documented in football fanzines since the mid 80s.

From the *Athletic News* to 'Sportuguese'

Talk about football has been a popular pastime since the game first became a spectator sport in the 1880s. This oral tradition continues today, the discussions revolving around the results, the prospects of the game the following week, and the general scrutiny of players, managers and the board. Talking about football has been an almost exclusive male domain, often practised in the 'patriarchy on the street corner' - the pub (Hey, 1986). The pub was a major site of 'cathectic relations' (Hearn, 1992, p.206) between men, providing an intimate space for drinking and chatting about sport. Social historians of football - Walvin (1975), Mason (1980), and Hutchinson (1982) - have all noted the relationships between football and pubs, a male oral tradition central to the game's popularity. This large, predominantly working class male, enthusiasm and interest in football was ripe for exploitation by the emerging popular press of the late nineteenth century. With the introduction of laws to provide free, secular and compulsory education, literacy became far more pervasive throughout the industrial workforce. Football became an indispensable sphere of newspaper coverage, mainly consisting of results and the following weekend fixtures which led to the development of an early football pools. A specialized sporting press was also developed to cater for the growing demand from an increasing football spectatorship eager to quench their thirst for this new form of 'sports knowledge'. The *Scottish Athletic Journal*, established in September 1882, came out weekly on Fridays and after a couple of years established sales in the region of 20,000 (Murray, 1984, p.47). The relationship between football, the press and the breweries was cemented through advertising. To sustain a large and popular readership the price of newspapers was kept to a minimum, the major source of income derived from advertisements. For instance, *The Football Pink 'Un* based in Birmingham at the turn of the century, included over four hundred advertisements from pub, hotel and restaurant proprietors in issues of the handbill in 1904 (Tischler,1981, p.78). Moreover, many club directors were wholesalers and retailers from the alcohol trade, which accentuated the differentiation between the middle-class owners of the popular culture industries and their customers who were predominantly working class (Mason 1980, Tischler 1981, Dunning et al 1988).

Of further interest here are the relationships between club directors, League and FA officials, and newspaper publishers, editors and writers. According to Tischler (1981), articles tended to be mere descriptions of the match, often unsigned or under a pseudonym, and 'promoting football as it was structured'. One exception to this blandness were editorials or special 'guest columns' which were written by football officials and directors. For example, J. J. Bentley, president of the Football League, vice-president of the FA and who had a managing interest in Manchester United, was editor of the Manchester based *Athletic News*. William McGregor, one of the founder members of the League and vice-president of Aston Villa, had a weekly column in Sunderland's *Football Echo* and Birmingham's *Sports Argus* (Tischler,1981, p.79). Some articles read like long academic discussions on football, for instance J. A. H.

Catton of the *Athletic News*, who went under the pseudonym 'Tityrus' or 'Athleo' (Fishwick, 1989, p.102). These cross-media/football interests (a small scale forerunner to contemporary media mogul/football relationships exemplified by the likes of Burlosconi the president of AC Milan) helped publicize and popularize the Football League, ensuring the hegemony of a new management class in the running of the game. There was often vilification for any player that stepped out of line, usually over wage disputes, the Maximum Wage Rule and the retain and transfer system proving to be useful tools for club management committees wanting players to accept their terms (Harding 1991). The sporting press carried little in the way of player profiles, especially with regard to their backgrounds or social and political interests outside the game. As Tischler observed about the apparent conservatism within the press and football hierarchy:

> While the Players Union received support in trade union and Labour party journals, the control of the popular sporting press by club directors and League and Association officials deprived players - and the labour movement as a whole - of a forum for the discussion of alternative methods of organizing professional football and worker recreation in general (Tischler, 1981, p.81).

Discussions about the behaviour and social patterns of spectators were also played out on the pages of the sporting press. Discourses in favour of the moral and social benefits of the 'amateur-ideal', usually propagated by the upper and middle classes, were still prevalent at the turn of the century. Their worries usually centred on the degradation caused by professional competitiveness, not only to the game as it was played, but also to the moral and physical well-being of spectators who were prone to the perceived dangers of drinking, smoking and gambling. Most of the formal barriers to professionalism had been relinquished due to the large support of northern clubs by local businessmen eager to patronize the development of the Football League. However, the gentleman-amateur, bourgeois element remained in control of the national apparatus of the game through the FA. C. A. Alcock, the FA's first Secretary, embodied such spirit against the pitfalls of professionalism which he saw as 'the evil to be repressed' (Tomlinson, 1991, p.27). What appears to have occurred in the early development of the professional game was a 'three way accommodation between classes' (Hargreaves, 1986, p.69) which saw local capital move into League football - capturing the loyalty of the working class - while the FA was controlled by an upper middle class still exerting an influence on the predominantly working class player, through the notions of 'sportsmanship' associated with the FA Cup and 'national pride' associated with playing for one's country. The popular press played a significant role in consolidating the structure of the League while maintaining the 'specialness' of the Cup competition which had its roots in the amateur traditions of the game. These discourses and practices pervaded the English game throughout its history and as Tomlinson argues:

> This has led to many clashes of values, of a classically patrician-plebeian kind, in which the old amateur/professional tensions have been relived (Tomlinson, 1991, p.26).

Moreover, these clashes and tensions can be traced through the history of football literature and journalism, which developed as the game and the mass-circulation media continued to expand and modernize, introducing new dichotomies.

The strong sense of parochialism felt among supporters of the newly formed professional clubs at the turn of the century helped to secure the hegemony of local businessmen in the running of clubs. Supporter involvement in the administrative side of clubs was minimal if not non-existent. There had been a history of spectators raising funds and organizing trips to football from the game's early beginnings and in the early part of the 20th Century more formal ties and recognition between supporters and clubs began to emerge. Watford SC (1911) and Crystal Palace SC (1912) are two of the earliest recorded supporters clubs which eventually led to the formation of the National Federation of Football Supporters Clubs in 1927 (R. Taylor, 1991). Many clubs began to put aside columns in the programme for the supporters' clubs but comment on any internal politics was strictly taboo, or would be censored. In 1934 the NFFSC produced its own newsletter entitled *The Supporter*, a monthly broadsheet that only managed to survive for two years. After the Second World War the *Football Supporters' Gazette* was launched, its objective "to create and foster enthusiasm in the parent club, to encourage greater support at the matches, and by raising of funds to financially assist the football clubs" (R. Taylor, 1991, p.120). The attempt to provide propaganda on behalf of the club could hardly be described as a radical move for change, indeed many supporters clubs became merely a subsidiary of the football club itself. As Taylor has argued, the Federation reflected the FA from which it sought recognition in its "middle-class propriety" and "distinct 'southern' and 'amateur' constituency" (1991, p.121).

The only outlet for public criticism of the local club was on the letters page of the local newspapers. These were common and often vociferous in their attack on the way football clubs were managed. For instance, the following letter, quoted by Taylor, appeared in the *Leicester Mercury* in 1921 suggesting:

> That a place should be found on the directorate for at least two members elected to represent the opinions of the very large band of supporters...The club is, properly speaking, an institution of the town and not a kind of private trading company, conducted at the whim of the few men who are at the moment immediately interested (R. Taylor, 1991, p.115).

As Taylor says, such a quote would not be out of place in contemporary fanzines.

Disquiet about the capitalist roots of professional football came from more radical quarters. The *Daily Worker*, the publication of the Communist Party, initially set out to expose the corrupt character of football as a 'boss sport', proposing an alternative of the Workers' Sports Movement (Jones, 1986). However, as football became increasingly popular and perceived as the working class sport, the *Worker* had to compromise its purist stance and even adopted language more in tune with the values of the market (Fishwick, 1989, p.104).

Football journalism in the local and national popular press was also moving apace with a growing market. By the 1930s with the mushrooming of young journalistic talent on the back pages of daily newspapers, the *Athletic News*, the football equivalent of *The Times*, had drastically lost its appeal and became defunct. Most local newspapers enjoyed a favourable relationship with the local club, access to 'behind the scenes' events helped establish a broader perspective for the football reader. However, the cozy relationship that many journalists developed in this respect, mediated their capacity to criticize the club too heavily. Players were still out of bounds, and any defamatory articles or letters were seen as destructive in terms of morale. Indirect criticism through the letters page was a means by which the press maintained contact with its readership, providing a vent for supporters grievances. The actual reporting of games also secured a commercial interest by being detailed and strong in local interest. The Saturday evening specials which were associated with local papers, printed on coloured sheets, giving them their names, invariably the *Football Pink* or the *Green 'Un*, published reports from various levels of local football.

From the inter-war years national newspapers were vying for position in the market. Football publicized itself on a national scale in a capacity far greater than ever before. Reporting of off the field activities reached new heights, the antics of football managers becoming a prime focus of football journalism. Managers gained a 'mystique' as their team tactics were increasingly seen by the press as the key to success. Editors believed circulation would increase as the amount of sports coverage increased and *The People* set new trends in "lively, aggressive, irreverent football reporting" (Fishwick, 1989, p.101). From humorous anecdotes to sensational stories, reports were designed to appeal to the inquisitive nature of the football supporter. A new style of journalism, imported from American boxing reporters, was taken up by the popular press. Fishwick notes that this new 'Sportuguese' - informal, jargon-ridden, and clichéd - was strongly identified with Trevor Wignall of the *Daily Express* in the late 20s and 30s. Fishwick contends:

What was happening therefore was that a style of reporting designed for a highly commercialised, violent, money-oriented American sport was being applied to a very different game in England. The image and linguistic images of football that the new journalists conveyed to the reader were changed accordingly, providing a dramatic contrast with those of the 1920s and before (Fishwick, 1989, p.106).

Football coverage was firmly rooted to the back page, full of 'action' photographs and satirical cartoons.

The rise of a football writing fraternity

According to Geoffrey Green (1974) "the span 1946 to 1959 provided the gateway to the vast expansion of the game that we know today". The centrality of the game is evocatively described in this passage from Ward and Alister's (1981) oral history of Barnsley FC between 1953-59:

> On Saturday evenings the Barnsley streets became a sea of *Green 'Un's* as the fanatics read the *Sheffield Star* reports. They met their wives and, depending on their mood after the match, took a night on the town, perhaps a meal at the bus station cafe and a visit to one of the eight cinemas or a dance-hall. Occasionally a man could be seen reading the *Green 'Un* behind his partner's back as they waltzed (Ward and Aister,1981, p.3).

In the aftermath of war and the prevailing hardship of rationing the demand for entertainment was greater than ever before. Football and its reportage helped to consolidate ideas of national honour and at the same time foster the eagerness for enjoyment of an increasingly optimistic British society. The 1950s saw notable changes in the structure of the game: the introduction of floodlights providing a new form of evening entertainment, the updating of equipment and the establishment of European club competition. The pressure for wages and status from the Players Union also increased as players themselves began to step into the limelight. Players like Blanchflower, Mathews, Finney, Lawton, and Edwards became the 'personalities' of the game but showed more sobriety than the 'star status' to be reached by the players of the late 60s (see Critcher, 1979, for his typology of professional footballers from the 1950s to the 1970s). The fashion for reporters to enter the dressing room greatly affected the changing perceptions of players and the transfer fee stories began to override traditional descriptions of the game which had rested on the adage of J. A. H. Catton of the *Athletic News* of reporting 'what happened, how it happened, and why it happened'.

Much of the fierce competition to find a newsworthy story from football was due to the saturation of the British popular newspaper market. As Wagg (1984) has argued a certain degree of 'occupational identity' grew among football correspondents, reflected by the Football Writers Association formed in 1947. The emerging popular style of football journalism was trivial, sensational, and highly opinionated. Football as melodrama was the convention of the day, a style that had developed with mass communication and the need to produce a condensed, selective form of presentation. It would not be unusual for over 200 reporters to attend the Cup Final and the 1954 World Cup attracted upwards of 1200 reporters (Ledbrooke and Turner, 1955). The broader processes in mass communications and literature were documented by Richard Hoggart (1957). He noted that the centralization and concentration of popular reading was characterized by fewer papers, written by newer journalists, with the "flat assumption that the lowest level of response and interest only is *de rigueur*", suggesting that "one doesn't read such papers; one looks at them" (Hoggart, 1957, p.203).

However, there were more learned and detailed approaches to football journalism which stood in stark contrast to their contemporaries in the nations' sporting press. Ladbrooke and Turner (1955) in their revised edition of *Soccer From The Press Box* believed that 'the man with the typewriter' had often lost sight of what his job was. They suggested that there are two ways of writing about football:

> You can watch the game as ninety minutes of sport and treat it as a piece of entertainment complete in itself. Or you can attempt to relate the match to all the football preceding it in eighty or ninety years of organised Association football. It is the view of the writers that every match, every transfer and every bit of legislation, have a place in the larger framework, and the notes which make up this and other chapters here are the result of thinking aloud over a number of years watching football in various parts of the world.

Furthermore:

> An experienced and skilled football reporter is presumably paid by his newspaper to tell of what he sees, and if his energies are primarily directed thus, he would seem to be going a long way towards earning his money as well as satisfying his readers.

There were other voices of discontent as the state of football and the style of the English game in general were seen to be in decline. A foreign correspondent on British sport, Willy Meisl, felt that the failure of British soccer in the post-war period - epitomized by England's first defeat on home soil in 1953 at Wembley and their heaviest defeat ever (7-1) in 1954, both at the mercy of Hungary - was due in some degree to the 'overstatement' and 'inflated' language of the nation's press. Born in Vienna, Meisl had moved to England to escape Hitler's Nazis, and writing for many journals including *World Sports* had subsequently developed a form of idealism and patriotism for English football. His ideals, and apprehension about his livelihood, led him to write *Soccer Revolution*, a book intended "to help save British soccer from drowning in an ocean of mediocrity" (1956, p.9). Meisl's dedication and allegiance to his profession is indicated in the following passage:

> To me journalism has always been as much a mission as a job, not basically different from a scientists, a general practitioner's or a vicars. We not only have to entertain, but also to inform and enlighten our readers. I am aware that if we fail to entertain them, we may lose them and the finest conviction, the most profound knowledge will have been wasted.

Such ethics were a rare commodity in the competitive world of sports journalism. Meisl illustrated the insularity of the British press, criticizing them for being conceited, "so certain that supremacy in Knowledge and legislation automatically goes with supremacy on the field" (1956, p.101).

Soccer Revolution was one of the many sports books published and distributed by the Sportsman's Book Club. The aim of the club was to promote access to books which epitomized the 'best' in sports writing. Hence, football books which appeared in the series aimed to improve the sports fans' knowledge and appreciation of the British game. In 1958 the club published *The Spectators Handbook* by J. B. Pick which reflected the 'improving' and 'middlebrow' approach taken up by the mail order company. The *Handbook* gave an introductory guide to watching football: the best vantage points from which to watch the pattern of play; the basic tactics to look out for; the essentials of a good team; and general information on the Football League. In many respects the *Handbook* reads like an FA coaching manual for spectators, or a television moralist's guide to respectable fan behaviour. To borrow Hoggart's (1957, p.185) phrase about 'middlebrow' writing of this period, the *Handbook* appeals to football supporters to be "serious without solemnity and cheerful without cheapness". This writing style saw spectatorship as a pastime as worthwhile as actually playing the sport, but maintained the ideals of being a 'good sport' - the good of the game was more important than local chauvinism - so that the tensions between professional spectator and amateur traditions were only partially compromised.

It can be seen, therefore, that two styles of writing and reading about football emerged in the immediate post-war period: those seeking to entertain and uncover the stories from 'behind the scenes' to sell newspapers in a highly competitive market; and those which sought to improve the game through extensive analysis of tactics and ethics, while keeping a tight reign on overt commercial interference in the game.

Football writing in the 'modern era'

Steve Redhead (1987) has characterized England's 1966 World Cup victory as the beginning of the 'modern football era'. This followed the ending of the maximum wage in 1961 and George Eastham's success of 1963 in getting the High Court to declare the retain and transfer system illegal. Football journalists certainly played their part in establishing this new era. The headlines of the *News Chronicle* in 1959 had demanded "Set the players free" as the belief in restricting the movement and living standards of players was no longer tenable. The amount of publicity afforded top players grew increasingly in the 1960s and there was a thawing of the 'high handed' attitude clubs had taken to the press. If the 1950s and early 60s had seen a certain amount of deference by players in their relationship with the press, the 'modern' era of the late 60s saw players flaunting their new found success, playing out the role of 'the star' (Critcher,1979). 'Beatlemania' in 1963 had set a new precedent in the way the press fed a phenomenon and a phenomenon fed the press. The chanting of Beatles songs on the terraces of Anfield, Liverpool exemplified the merging of football and 'pop' culture and a new era of fandom. George Best personified the crossover, appearing as frequently in the music press as the football pages of national newspapers. Best's magical skill and ostentatious manner was ripe for the media exploitation which in turn fed the young Irish footballers' own dreams of personal success (excess). As Hopcraft writing in 1968 at the dawn of a new football era ironically commented on Best's new acquaintances:

> For one moment I thought I saw Georgie collecting somebody's autograph; actually he was taking a pop singers' address (Hopcraft, 1968, p.20).

This period of football journalism, post 1966, was characterized by the saturation of writing and publications on the game - the majority of it aimed at a young audience. A traditional football fare for boys was epitomized by *Roy of the Rovers*, the comic strip that charted the rise of Roy Race of Melchester Rovers into a cult football personality. But it was not long before 'real life' characters were subjected to the same form of media treatment. George Best, Rodney Marsh, Tony Currie, and Alan Hudson are just a selection of players that regularly appeared in the publications *Goal* and *Shoot*, two of the most successful teen-magazines, later to be joined by *Match*. Such publications, filled with glossy photographs and innocuous articles, were part of a broader commercialization of football which aimed to merchandise every possible artefact emblazoned with the names of players or clubs. The football fraternity became far more weary of its own publicity - hence the increasing proliferation of biographies which were of the 'my story' genre - claiming to tell the 'reality' behind the fog of tabloid press reportage. The tabloids had a tendency to create hostilities within the football world by 'naming names'. For instance, before the 1970 World Cup in Mexico, Bobby Moore the captain of England's 1966 winning side, attracted increasing speculation and criticism from certain sections of the press for being more concerned with his business interests than playing football for his country. Moore made a retort in the suitably named biography *England! England!* suggesting:

> People are always ready to put you on a pedestal. Once they have put you there they are quick to try to knock you off it ... My so called business interests never have and never will interfere with my football in any shape or form (Moore, 1970, p.18).

Moore, in fact, was one of many players of the late 60s and early 70s that proved football and business could be blended together while retaining some form of professional respectability. The football player as businessman was to be taken to new heights later in the 70s by Kevin Keegan who in the words of Wagg (1984, p.145) was: "... football's first clone - a persona economically fashioned with a huge audience of consumers in mind".

Other players had found success in broadcasting, most notably Jimmy Hill and Bob Wilson. Journalists themselves exploited the opportunities available in the broadening football 'mediascape'. Michael Parkinson who was a sports columnist for *The Times* among others, developed his own 'personality' status by hosting his own chat show, which brought together the disparate worlds of sport (mainly cricket and football), film, literature, and politics for the sake of 'light entertainment' on Saturday nights, invariably after *Match of the Day*. Parkinson was an avid Barnsley fan and although writing in the 'modern era', often drifted into nostalgia to prove his northern working class credentials as the following passage from his book *Football Daft* illustrates:

> Even now it's easy to switch my mind back twenty years to the days when we caught the bus and made the five mile journey into Barnsley to see the Reds play. The bus was always crowded with men in hairy overcoats and flat caps, smelling of woodbines and last night's beer (Parkinson, 1971).

In 1973 Parkinson edited an anthology of soccer with Willis Hall entitled *Football Report*, compiled for the 'Goaldiggers Trust' a charity made up of 'celebrities' many of whom were football journalists or had written about football. Noticing the merging of football with other spheres of media and culture, Parkinson and Hall wrote in the introduction:

> ... reviewing the area of choice it seems remarkable how soccer nowadays cuts through every strata of our society and stimulates writers and artists in every field of what might loosely be called the communications industry. Soccer has always had its good reporters, men who have observed the game with style and perception, but it is only recently that it has come to be used as an everyday source for the dramatist, novelist and song writer. Football today is no longer the palliative for the working class, it

is a well-tapped source of humour, drama and conflict for all of us to enjoy (Hall and Parkinson, eds., 1973, p.14).

The process described above corresponds favourably with Ian Taylor's (1971) theory of 'bourgeoisification' of the game during this period, where watching football became a passive 'spectacle' to be appreciated - a shift in the 'soccer consciousness'. It is easy to be over critical of these processes; however, the synopsis given by Parkinson and Hall gives an early glimpse of the implosion of traditional meanings around football, which has since been characterized by the crossing of perceived boundaries between 'high' and 'low' culture. Parkinson's interviews with the football 'stars' celebrated - often with inordinate banality - the new found success and riches to be had by professional sportsmen (rarely were sporting guests female). His show gained immoderate success hand in hand with the esteem and persona of his sporting guests who were no doubt scheduled to appear on *Pro-Celebrity Golf* or *Superstars* the following week. All this exemplifies the media processes geared towards constructing mythological star status for a select number of footballers, over and above the adoration they received from the terraces, which required a new form/style of football reporter/ presenter.

More orthodox football journalism did continue through into the 'modern era', carrying on in the footsteps of Geoffrey Green and John Arlott who had established themselves in the 50s. Hopcraft's (1968) *The Football Man* is still one of the most compelling football books ever written. Conjuring up the full fascination of football and why "it engages the personality" the book was signing off a particular age of the game. Hopcraft himself left the press box to concentrate on being an author and playwright. By the 1970s the most prestigious football writing came from the back pages of the Sunday papers: Brian Glanville of *The Sunday Times*; Tony Pawson and Hugh McIlvenney of *The Observer*; and Danny Blanchflower of the *Sunday Express*. *The Glory Game* by Hunter Davies (1972), who also worked for *The Sunday Times*, was *the* inside story of this period. It was an account of his one year with Spurs enabling a 'fly on the wall' type documentary. Unfortunately, *The Glory Game* failed to deliver the kind of incisive understanding of the upwardly-mobile footballer of the period. In a scathing review of the book for *New Society* in October 1972, Ian Taylor argued that Davies' "clever and impressionistic journalism" was mainly concerned with providing an "amusing or colourful brand of reportage". As Taylor commented:

> The result is a truncated resentful kind of impressionism which tells us little about the 'obvious' changes in the structures or culture of professional soccer.

The style of the Sunday paper football journalist was often a 'middlebrow' version of the football gossip, so heavily relied upon by the tabloid press. The finest exponent of hyperbole was *The Sun* which, born out of the 'swinging sixties' in November 1969, was 'ruthlessly downmarket'. Dragging other tabloid coverage of football down with them in the never-ending search for controversy and indignation *The Sun* carved out an intensified vocabulary: 'Sunspeak', which entered the national consciousness utilizing emotion not reason. As Wagg (1991, p.223) has pointed out, the emotive journalism of *The Sun* and its main competitors is "concerned with fame - the Known-ness of people - and the interplay between the public world of the 'known' and the private". In the early 70s, with television heightening the profile of certain players, transfer fees escalated rapidly and football immersing itself in the entertainment business, *The Sun* did not seek explanations but publicity, engineering an "imaginary dialogue with a generalised other: the *Sun* reader" (Wagg, 1991, p.223). This often meant 'slagging off' players and managers for failing to deliver, usually because of greed and immersing such narratives in nationalistic discourses that emphasized Britain's (or England's) role in developing the game of football. *The Sun* attempted to perform the journalistic equivalent of the professional foul every time a player, manager or whole team 'slipped up', had a 'nightmare', got 'smashed' or were caught with their trousers down! As the stakes increased so did the pressures upon players who were increasingly alienated from the daily running of the game and their media image.

It is because of these pressures and alienating forces that Eamon Dunphy, professional footballer with 2nd. Division Millwall, wrote a diary of his experiences during the 1973-74 season to undermine tabloid lies and counter-lies that pervaded the game in this period. *Only A Game?* was the most incisive account of football from within the industry, expressing both wit and sadness. His account of the uneasy and contradictory relationship between players and football journalists is worth quoting at length. Its sentiment still holds true today:

> Whereas theatre critics and film critics do know what the mechanics of a production are, most football writers don't. So players tend to despise journalists. On the other hand, players are flattered by their attention. Flattered by the idea that this guy has come along especially to write about them. So you have contempt and at the same time a slight awe at seeing your name in print. And players tend to have a special face that they show to journalists...With a journalist a player shows another side to the one he shows his colleagues. Journalists and players have an uneasy relationship really. It doesn't work very well. Journalists always have their preconceptions, their angles. And they then want to try and make the player say the things they want him to say. And it is all too easy for journalists to do this. They don't go into a story to discover but to substantiate preconceived ideas... What is important in the game is how it is played. How people are motivated to do the bad things, and how they are motivated to do the good things. And what is going on at a club at a particular time. What stage the club is at in the process of success and failure. How a game went, or why something happened. You very rarely read that. They personalise that, and it becomes a game of personalities. And if there aren't enough personalities, they create them. And that is destructive (Dunphy, 1976, p.117-118).

Dunphy's disillusionment with the internal workings and politics of the football industry is typical of an enthusiast, who once inside that industry, has to put aside childhood dreams and preconceptions, to replace them with a degree of cynicism. Today, Dunphy is himself a journalist, based in Ireland and still holding no punches when it comes to his opinion of the game (for example, his criticism of Jack Charlton's managership of the Irish national side in Italia '90).

Dunphy was afforded the space to develop his journalistic talents, along with other budding journalists and writers, in 'Football's Alternative Paper': *Foul*. *Foul*, whose name parodied those of glossy football magazines, ran from 1972 -1976. In all, 34 issues were published and its circulation grew to around 10,000. It is the 70s nearest equivalent to a football fanzine. The magazines' irreverent style owed much to the satirical movement that developed out of the 60s, epitomized by the likes of *Beyond The Fringe*. Steve Tongue, Alan Stewert, Stan Hey, Andrew Nicholds, Peter Ball, Chris Lightbown and cartoonist Bill Tidy were the magazines' main contributors. Tongue and Stewert had begun the magazine as undergraduate students at Cambridge. After several typewritten editions its style, production and distribution were enhanced when it was published by the parent company of *Private Eye*, which traded in political satire and also had its roots in Oxbridge. Many of *Foul*'s contributors were already working in the media and it had gained financial support from Tim Rice. *Foul* railed against all that the football establishment stood for, the irresponsibility and sensationalism of the press, the lack of creative and imaginative play due to overt 'professionalism' by teams like Leeds United, and the unsympathetic, backward beliefs held in football boardrooms towards the game and supporters in particular. Looking back at why *Foul* emerged when it did, Chris Lightbown suggested:

> To understand *Foul* you have to understand the Fifties. It's virtually impossible for anyone who wasn't around then to imagine quite how boring this country was. Really, I think the motivation behind *Foul* was that football had simply not assimilated any of the social or cultural changes of the sixties. It was in a complete time warp. That's why it was called 'The Alternative Football Paper' (cited in *The Face, 1987*).

Steve Redhead (1987 and 1991) has documented *Foul*'s investigative intervention into the politics of professional football, particularly its accusations against the PFA which rested on the union's weakness (PFA = Pretty Feeble Altogether) and its exploitation by key officials. *Foul*, and its short lived protégé *The Leveller*, gave rhetorical support to a flagging 'freedom' campaign for professional footballers, but as Redhead (1991) has argued an emerging affluent consumer society supported by a global mass media made fighting for players rights increasingly problematic and contradictory. With regard to press treatment of football, *Foul* lampooned the incessant triviality of tabloid journalism by plundering quotes from newspapers, unmasking the soft-edged bonhomie between journalists and football managers and generally 'taking the piss' in a manner which reflected many young, white male middle class 'alternative' attitudes of the day.

In a review of the 1972-73 season the magazine called football journalism's hypocrisy into question by asking "HAS THE PRESS TAKEN ITS RESPONSIBILITIES MORE SERIOUSLY?". This brought a resounding 'no' and the statement:

> The prospect of the press improving its coverage of soccer is bleak, unless readers get as bored with the endless pages of tat as they appear to be with the sport itself (from *The Foul Book of Football No. 1, 1976*, p.29).

This pessimistic outlook, written at a time of drastically falling attendance figures, foreshadowed the hyper-sensationalism and banality of the tabloids in the 80s. Phil Shaw (1989) suggests that *Foul*'s format "left a blueprint for the next generation" which to a degree is true. Many of *Foul*'s targets - Jimmy Hill and Leeds United for starters - are much the same as those vilified by contemporary fanzines. However, the differences that fanzines have from *Foul* are twofold: firstly, fanzines are motivated by a 'do it yourself' ethos which owes much to 'punk' and influenced large areas of youth culture something the writers in *Foul* had never been subject to; and secondly, a far greater conviction among a broader section of fans after the tragedies of the 80s to create a forum for the expression of grievances and fan politics. Tom Baker (*The Face, 1987*) believed "the general tone of the magazine forces the reader to view it as a precursor to punk" yet it wasn't until the mid 80s that punk philosophy began to influence fan productivity to create Goldberg's 'Radical Football Faction'. Indeed, Mike Ticher, founding member of *When Saturday Comes* admitted to his ignorance of *Foul* until after he had published the first issue of his fanzine and subsequently received copies of the 70s magazine from one of his readers. Ticher then produced his own eulogy to *Foul* with the book *Foul: Best of Football's Alternative Paper, 1972-76* in 1987. *Foul*'s demise in 1976, due to libel, occurred at a time when football's 'modern' era was truly embedded - soon there would be million pound deals and plastic pitches. On the terraces fans became subject to increasing surveillance, segregation and separation. As Ian Taylor (1989) has argued this social and political restructuring of grounds ultimately led to Hillsborough, a disaster that could have happened at any number of stadiums. Furthermore, the game of the late 70s and the early 80s was "a different ball game from the heady days of flower power" (Redhead, 1987, p.34) which *Foul*'s pages so acerbically documented.

3   Waiting for the great leap forward (2): The genealogy of fanzines

Punk fanzines

The social and cultural changes that occurred just at the time of *Foul*'s demise provides another thread in the genealogy of fanzines. The cultural signs are not from football but pop music and the disjuncture that was occurring within this realm of popular culture. The implosive nature of punk on the music industry and popular culture in general in 1976 is of specific significance to the emergence of music and football fanzines in the 80s. Introducing their 'scrapbook' collections of football fanzines Phil Shaw (1989), Martin Lacey (1989) and John Robinson (1989) all pay homage to punk fanzines *Ripped & Torn*, *Sniffin' Glue* and *48 Thrills* among others, as influencing the former's "generic moniker" and "key production components" as Shaw (1989) termed it. However, more than lip service needs to be paid to the punk ancestry of fanzines to fully understand and appreciate this particular youth culture's legacy, influence and difference from the contemporary scene. This requires analysing the conditions within which punk fanzines and ideology operated and, subsequently, how post-punk ideas and styles fed into football fan culture in the 80s.

Documenting the rise and fall of the Sex Pistols in his book *England's Dreaming*, Jon Savage has the following to say about the new youth cult and urban reality of 1976:

> Punk announced itself as a portent with its polysemy of elements drawn from the history of youth culture, sexual fetish wear, urban decay and extremist politics. Taken together, these elements had

no conscious meaning but they spoke of many things; urban primitivism; the breakdown of confidence in a common language; the availability of cheap, second-hand clothes; the fractured nature of perception in an accelerating, media-saturated society; the wish to offer up the body as a jumble of meaning (Savage, 1991, p.230).

It was the idea of recycling which marked out the new pop aesthetic. Fanzines provided graphics and typography that were homologous with punk's subterranean and anarchic style. The language was working class, the text jumbled up with typing errors and grammatical mistakes. Articles were usually based on reviews of bands or interviews with renowned punks of the 'inner circle' (i.e. Vicious, Rotten, Siouxsie, McLaren). Production was cheap, small scale - which was aided and abetted by the technological development of photocopiers. Savage remembers that the point was access, exemplified by the fanzines' "access aesthetic".

The access and enthusiasm to produce fanzines enabled a definition of punk from those submerged within the culture. To be more precise, it enabled a multitude of definitions, scrambling the definitions and commentary in the tabloid and music press. The irony of using 'ransom-note' lettering in punk literature - individual letters cut out of newspapers - first used in A4 handbills to advertise the Sex Pistols, emphasized the subversion of the media and a playing with its form. Unprofessional, unglossy, unreadable at any length - fanzines drew on punks' politics of rupture, partly engineered by Situationist inspired Malcolm McLaren but highly induced by a sense of boredom in a passive English society. Punks radical everyday style - in music, fashion and fanzines - created a chaos to wake England from its dreaming slumber. As Iain Chambers says:

Here were the slogans daubed on the cultural fatigues of punk's battle dress: DESTROY. ANARCHY. Here, a passive public was displaced by those who had constructed a 'situation'. Here were the 'livers' seeking to break the invisible fetters of a complacent environment. The Dadaist logic of sucking in the trivia, the rubbish and the castoffs of the world and then stamping a new meaning on the chaotic assemblage was there in both punk's music and sartorial regime (Chambers, 1985, p.182).

By October 1976, Carolyn Coon in the *Melody Maker* had coined the phrase 'do it yourself' as central to punk ideology. A fanzine called *Bam Balam* which covered sixties music showed the way for anyone who wanted to produce their own magazine. But it was Mark P's *Sniffin' Glue* that signalled the entrance of punk fanzines, its name taken from a Ramones album. Using a photocopier at his girlfriend's dad's office, Mark P. approached the fanzine "like a project in school" (Savage, 1991, p.201). Defining itself as 'FOR PUNKS', *Sniffin' Glue* was joined by Paul Morley's *Out There*, Toni D's *Ripped & Torn* from Glasgow and numerous other publications which found their way into an alternative network built up by touring punk bands and the rise of independent record shops. Punks' excess, polarization and inherent violence, attempted to produce itself outside the established media and cultural industries. The do it yourself philosophy, inverting traditional producer/consumer paradigms, formed a critique and instances of opposition to typical capitalist social relations. Fanzines communicated and constructed punk, with particular social vocabularies and ideological formulations. Again, this time referring to his diary of September 1977, Savage comments:

> Fanzines are the perfect expression - cheaper, more instant than records. Maybe THE medium. A democratization too - if the most committed 'new wave' is about social change then the best fanzines express this. Perhaps most importantly outside saturated London, they provide a vital function as a base/co-ordination point of the local scene. And that means Ilford as much as Glasgow. Eventually new impetus, reinterpretation will come from there (quoted in Savage, 1991, p.401).

The linguistic and production styles of British fanzines were to be copied across the globe in the US, for instance *Slash* from Los Angeles in 1977 which helped foster local punk bands in the late 70s and early 80s (James, 1988).

Did football have any specific relation to punk? Regional differences - which form such a solid part of football fandom - did inflect the London centredness of punk. Mancunian punk mixed up ethics and ideals of autonomy with a strong sense of regional identity, and a passing nod to the football terrace. Slaughter and the Dogs in particular showed a different attitude to the fashion conscious punks elsewhere. Coming from Wythenshawe, a council estate in South Manchester, Slaughter and the Dogs enacted the violent rhetoric of the mid 70s Stretford End through punk music. The Fall, also from Manchester, gave their tirade about football with 'Kicker Conspiracy', shooting the video at Turf Moor, Burnley. During punk's swan song Serious Drinking recorded the football love song *Love On the Terrraces*. Another link between punk and football came from The Cockney Rejects with their punk version of the West Ham football anthem 'I'm Forever Blowing Bubbles'. A more sinister punk/football crossover came with the 'return' of a skinhead style which appeared at gigs involving the likes of Sham 69, a band that attracted a hardcore punk following. The skinhead style and its association with football had originally faded in the early 70s but resurfaced in the late 70s in a far more chauvinistic mode. The 'swastika' had been plundered by punk in a playful show of subversion, but its extreme political connotations were taken up by neo-fascist groups eager to extend their influence on white working class male youth, particularly on the football terraces. By 1979 punk had metamorphosed into something quite different from its early period of social unrest. The Anti-Nazi League and Rock Against Racism consumed much of the energy of punk, *Temporary Hoarding* an anti-racist publication the last punk fanzine to influence the development of music and football fanzines of the mid to late-80s. However, movements against neo-fascism in the streets and through music failed to turn their attention to the inroads the ultra-Right were attempting to make within football.

The End and the soccer casuals

Punk had signalled, in its own anarchic manner, the end of the post-war consensus, its vision of freedom to be "swamped by New Right power politics and the accompanying value systems" (Savage, 1991, p.541) However, it is a different narrative, that of the soccer casual, which appeared just when punk was fracturing which provides the next thread in the genealogy of football fanzines. Redhead (1991a) has excavated the ties between youth cultural styles and football culture which were epitomized by the casuals in this period. The influence of 'Bowie boys' from the mid 70s, the remnants of mod from the mid 60s and punks 'apocalyptic mood', combined with British football club success in European competition to provide a complex, subversive challenge to traditional notions of masculinity on the football terrace. The desire to wear designer labels and 'top' sports gear exclusively from the continent fed into sharpened regional rivalries which gave us 'chaps' (London), 'scallies' (Merseyside) and 'perries' (Manchester) among others. It is from this fashion conscious youth culture that an influential model for contemporary fanzines, *The End*, arose.

The End came out of Merseyside, capturing the mood of the early 80s terrace culture, and its format can be seen as a forerunner to the plethora of football fanzines that emerged in the mid to late 80s. Originally co-edited by Phil Jones and Peter Hooton (who went on to be the lead singer for the fanzines 'in house' band The Farm) *The End* billed itself as "The North's Finest Music Paper". In Issue 3 of the fanzine in 1982, Jones put the record straight for any unsuspecting intellectual bores with pretentious musical taste by stating:

> ... this is supposed to be a humorous music mag. And scousers are supposed to have a sense of humour. If it's a serious, no-nonsense music mag you want, there's quite a few other mag's around that will cater for your taste.

With an initial print run of 500 in 1981 *The End* developed a loyal following and by the last issue was selling in the region of 4500 and commanding cult status. The fanzine was designed for fellow 'scallies' who shared a similar taste in music, football and fashion. These tastes were by no means unified but a Liverpool night-club called Checkmate became the focus for a particular post-punk football fan sensibility between 1979-81. As Pete Naylor suggests in his retrospective article 'In Search of the Scally' (*Sounds*, March 1991) this Merseyside style had much to do with Liverpool and Everton's success in Europe during this period:

> With Merseyside fans having more chance than most to travel abroad, rare clothes and training shoes made their way back with numerous light-fingered individuals. This resulted in some unfortunates being accommodated at the expense of various European justice ministries, but also in a fabulous array of clothing at the match.

The End charted the lifestyle of "Liverpool's football following scallies" with articles like 'Are You A Real Scal?' (Issue 6), a dictionary of 'Liverpool Things' (Issue 3), guides to the 'Local Scene' and the perennial 'Ins and Outs' page which was to be copied by many fanzines in later years. As in all subcultures definitions of inclusion were accompanied by definitions of exclusion. Many articles 'took the piss' out of opposition fans, in particular 'Woollybacks' from Leeds and Yorkshire. As with most contemporary fanzines a lot of *The End*'s material relied on contributions from readers and it was on the Letters Page that fan rivalries were most prominently played out. The fanzine attracted attention from fans across the country which was boosted after it received attention in the mainstream music press. The majority of these letters boasted about the success or prowess of particular football casual crews each trying to outstrip the other, often with fictional wind-ups and frequently disputing who wore what and when. The vociferous and sometimes violent nature of these dialogues led to the misguided belief that *The End* was a hooligan publication. Yet as Redhead says in his analysis of the fanzine:

> ... it constituted an important intervention in football and fashion 'street' politics in a decade when 'style' came to signify a burgeoning affluence amongst the young upwardly mobile ('yuppie'). A different kind of sexual politics was being proffered here, offering new identities for young males interested in the 'holy' trinity of soccer, pop and clothes (Redhead, 1991a, p.152).

It was the identification with working class culture and in particular life on a deprived housing estate - such as Cantril Farm - that gave *The End* its political bite at a time when Thatcherism was in its full ascendancy. For this reason, despite defamatory articles about 'woolies', the fanzine openly defended socialist struggles like the miners strike of the mid 80s. More parochially, local working class heroes like the fictional (?) 'Yozzer Hughes' from Alan Bleasdale's *Boys From The Blackstuff* (Vol. 9), the Grant family from Channel 4's *Brookside* (Vol. 15) and comedian Alexi Sayle (Vol. 14) adorned the front covers of the fanzine. As another co-editor Mick Potter explained to Pete Naylor in an unpublished article 'The World Of *The End*':

> *The End* was a first. Most mags were student oriented and

alienated working class people's pastimes like the match and the alehouse. That had never really been touched on in the way we did in *The End*, probably because they'd never experienced it. A lot of working class people identified with us.

The idea that working class lads could produce something on their own - conduct interviews, write skit articles, draw cartoons, etc. - was novel and gained respect from their peers many of whom were later to be inspired by the fanzine. Again as Potter suggested to Pete Naylor:

People would ask us who did the interviews. I'd say 'me and Peter' and they'd be amazed. Just the idea that someone from a working class area was writing a magazine. We used to get lads from the match passing us poems, but saying 'don't use my name'. They were people who'd never written before in their lives. We used to get loads of poems, they knew there was a good chance of *The End* using it. They wanted to be associated with us.

The influence of *The End* on the explosion of fanzines that occurred after 1985 can easily be overstated, but there are specific instances where the fanzines' style and approach to the music, youth and football crossover were adopted. *Boy's Own* which appeared in the late 80s owed much to *The End* and the London fanzine editors Andy Weatherall and Terry Farley, who became central DJ-producers in late 80s club culture, eventually paid homage to Hooton and his band The Farm by producing their 'hit' singles 'Groovy Train' and 'All Together Now' in 1991. Back in Liverpool Pete Naylor began *What's The Score?*. Beginning strictly as a football fanzine, by September 1991 it exhibited many of *The End*'s characteristics (including the services of Mick Potter), in a somewhat glossier format, carrying more articles on music and clubbing than football and including numerous references to The Farm. However, as Naylor admits himself *The End*:

... was a rare original voice in what was, until near the end, a fairly dull and destructive decade. Often copied, *The End* will never be equalled.

Thatcherism and cultural politics

The politics of this destructive decade of the 1980s to which Naylor refers is crucial to an understanding of the changing nature of the football terrace and the subsequent rise of football fanzines. Thatcherism was an attempt to 'clear the way' for a new hegemony, based on financial independence, 'enterprise culture' and a shifting state policy that moved away from consent towards coercion. Cultural Marxist attempts to document the emerging conjuncture in Britain, often on the pages of *Marxism Today*, defined Thatcherism as a form of 'authoritarian populism' which pointed to a shift in the relations of force (see Hall 1988, and Gamble 1988). Capitalism's dynamic included the restructuring of cultural relations most visibly enacted by new youth cultures in the mid 80s consumer boom and the rise of the 'yuppie'. Furthermore, Thatcherism managed to gain populist consent for policies aimed to curb the 'enemy within', based around apparently non-political issues of race, law and order, permissiveness and social anarchy. However, Thatcherism's model of reconstruction, towards a new social regime, was an 'imaginary modernity' (Chambers 1990) its vision indebted to a backward-looking sense of the national heritage and family values.

The early to mid 80s saw continual repressive and authoritarian discourses engaged on popular culture. Football fans increasingly became subject to authoritarian measures in an attempt by the state to control unruly behaviour, images of violence being fuelled by the sensationalism of the press who continually instigated 'moral panics' about events occurring within football fan culture they could not begin to grasp. The Left's analysis of what was occurring within football fan culture was equally inept at comprehending the contradictory nature of early 80s terrace culture, the conventional view of deviance seeing youthful social unrest as a sign of a 'politics of resistance' to the regime of the New Right. Dave Robins (1984) story of the "youth Ends", *We Hate Humans,* painted a pessimistic picture of working class youth who were subject to the state's attempt to modify 'anti-social' behaviour through Youth Training Schemes. Robins sought to look behind the political lies and promises of affluent economic futures which were proffered up by the Thatcher Government for an increasingly disillusioned teenage population. In his 'End Piece' he argues:

So far organized youth resistance to unemployment has been minimal. But what happens if a whole generation discovers it has been in training for nothing? (Robins, 1984, p.156).

What such radical Marxist critiques failed to comprehend in the early to mid 80s was the fact that youth subcultures do not organically equate with a sense of counter culture or resistance to capitalist modes of production or consumption. Instead of a masculine parade of spectacle and outrage - predominantly associated with 'football hooliganism' since the late 60s - what has emerged, specifically since punk, are post-subcultural styles which produce multiple resistances that have as much to do with consumption as paradoxical ideas of youth counter-culture and opposition. Redhead has argued in relation to pop music:

What, in practice, we witnessed in the 1980s was the break-up not simply of former theoretical traditions (or master and meta-narratives) about the emancipatory potential of youth in the West, but the disintegration and restructuring of those formations (rock culture, youth culture) which were produced as their object. 'Authentic' subcultures were produced by subcultural theories, not the other way around (Redhead, 1990, p.25).

Such an argument does not intend to imply that we all became 'Thatcher's children' with rebellious styles disappearing into a mass of neo-conservative youth or 'hyper-conformity' but merely acknowledges the multiple discourses which frame contemporary youth culture. As suggested earlier in documenting the rise of *The End* and soccer casuals, youth styles in the 80s showed an ambiguous relationship with the hegemonic project of 'Thatcherism'. The casual style gave the appearance of wealth through its emphasis on expensive 'designer' menswear and sportswear hiding starker urban 'realities' of recession and industrial decay.

There did emerge in the 80s conscious attempts to forge new constituencies amongst youth to oppose the cultural politics of Thatcherism. Red Wedge, supported by an array of pop artists including Billy Bragg, Paul Weller, and The Redskins, attempted to raise awareness of contemporary political issues among young people. However, its attempt to capture the imagination of Britain's youth in a fight against Thatcherism, with its almost pious form of 'political pop' failed miserably as the Tory victory in 1987 was put down to its capture of young voters. But the mid 80s did see a new mood in the cultural politics of youth which came from a concern for ecology and a sense of the "Family of Man". Band Aid, and subsequent 'Aid' campaigns that followed, generated a mass 'popular movement' (representing world democracy, traditions of co-operation, mutual assistance and collective action) polarized against bureaucracy and individualism (the Us against Them mentality). Dick Hebdige (1988, p.222) argued that by resurrecting a "sense of possibility and common interest" the Aid phenomenon articulated a viable cultural politics for the 80s. Hebdige suggested:

> In this way we might say that the ultimate beneficiaries of Band Aid may well be us (not Them/as well as Them) in so far as a more enabling and more open handed version of "the public" and the "public interest" is once again available, circulating unconstrained (and uncontaminated) by party political affiliations and yet providing an alternative version of - a means of yearning beyond - the appetitive and paranoid versions of human motivation and human worth carried in the Thatcherite and Reaganite visions (Hebdige, 1988, p.220).

This particular brand of protest or 'political pop' did raise anger from more radical political commentators complaining about the capricious nature of some of the performers involved whose depth of loyalty to particular global issues were questioned (see for instance, Chumbawumba's LP, *Pictures of Starving Children*). But it is the (re)connection between the image and the 'real' that is of importance when trying to capture the essence of what Band Aid and the emerging eco-perspective meant within cultural politics.

Within football, tragedies at Heysel and Bradford in 1985 (and later Hillsborough in 1989) were beamed live into living rooms across the country. Immediate reactions to these events were couched in discourses of 'law and order' and 'hooliganism'. However, in spite of pessimistic pronouncements on the future of English football by the game's administrators and Tory rhetoric which fatalistically moved towards banning the game altogether, the tragedies provoked resolve and conviction amongst fans and 'ordinary people', who were clearly moved by these tragedies, to enact change within the game and alter the damaged public perception of the game in the 80s.

In August 1985 Rogan Taylor, a Liverpool supporter who had never voluntarily been in an organization in his life, set up the Football Supporters Association in direct response to the Heysel tragedy. In an interview in the aftermath of the 95 deaths at Hillsborough in 1989, Taylor remarked why the FSA was formed:

> I was actually writing something saying that one way of looking at Heysel is that the crowd is now totally alienated from the game; that what you see in the purple faces on the pitch is an image of the alienation of the supporters from every aspect of the game bar watching and paying for it (*Marxism Today*, September 1989).

Herein lies the conscious connection between the image and the reality of everyday life which has been instrumental in developing not only the FSA but also the plethora of football fanzines. By the 1985/86 season, after the tragedies at Bradford, Heysel and Birmingham where a teenage boy was crushed to death by a collapsing wall, football's image had reached an all time low and a heightened, authoritarian regime of policing was introduced to control supporters who were all treated as potential troublemakers. A feeling of guilt amongst many 'respectable' fans compounded the difficulty of protesting against such harsh measures. It was almost a case of self-censorship as talking about football and identifying yourself as a football fan was something hard to be proud of. The poet and *News On Sunday* columnist Attila The Stockbroker was later to argue:

> ... for our loyalty we get treated like criminals, herded around like cattle and abused by 'respectable citizens' (i.e. right wing, birdwatching, trainspotting, Paul Daniels-loving, Two Ronnies-adoring, football-hating morons in armchairs). Semi-literate hacks in brain-dead newspapers write about us in terms which suggest we are all collectively responsible for the Heysel disaster. Politicians use us as scapegoats, and the police as guinea-pigs for their latest crowd control techniques; they then make the clubs we support pay for the privilege - unlike Rupert Murdoch, who got his scab plant at Wapping protected for free - I wonder why? (*NSM*, December 1987).

But it was the investment of time, money and emotion into football by fans which proved to be a motivating factor the emergence of what Adrian Goldberg termed the 'Radical Football Faction'. In January 1986 Goldberg from Selly Oak, Birmingham, produced *Off The Ball* which set out to campaign on behalf of disgruntled fans. In Issue 1 his opening editorial began as follows:

> We won't be treated like idiots any more. We being "ordinary" supporters of mainly ordinary clubs, who are sick of being portrayed as morons in the press, tired of being patronised by television's lifeless coverage of a great sport, and most of all angry at being manipulated by tyrannical directors and administrators who, in their eagerness to "modernise" our game, show all the rationality of headless chickens.

And continued:

> For the true football fan, this really is the time for action. If players, managers and directors of the vast majority of clubs are too frightened of the big boys, or too shocked to react to superleague threats, then we are not.

Steve Beauchampe (who had "a hairstyle to be reckoned with") was another of the original contributors to *Off The Ball* providing a technical, photographic and artistic input. He emphasized the fanzines roots in the 'alternative' music and fanzine scene. He says:

> The main inspiration for *Off The Ball* was punk and the fanzine scene. Most of us were playing in small-time bands - none of us had had any writing published anywhere else (*The Face, 1987*).

Post-punk tastes in music and fashion in the mid 80s had blossomed into 'indie pop' which developed a postmodern pastiche of the 1960s counter culture with bands like Jesus and Mary Chain and The Pastels who were the subject of fanzines which helped to reinvigorate a flagging music fanzine culture. One of the most prominent of these fan magazines was *Debris* which came from the North West and was edited by Dave Haslam, DJ and joint owner of independent record company Play Hard. *Debris*, which began in 1983, addressed in a politically acerbic manner the contours of 80s youth and pop culture which were railing against the Thatcher government.

Bands themselves were beginning to turn their attention to football as a central part of everyday life. Most notably Half Man Half Biscuit who affectionately wormed their way into the hearts of many football/music lovers with numerous sessions on John Peels' night-time Radio 1 programme with songs like 'All I want for Christmas is a Dukla Prague away kit' a reference to the table football game Subbuteo and 'I was a teenage armchair Honved fan' a reference to the pre-Heysel days when English teams in European competition were an ever present feature of mid-week sports programmes. Their debut LP *Back In The DHSS* was an ironic and wry political statement of life on the dole in the 80s. Other bands to celebrate their love of football in their music and record sleeves were: I, Ludicrous with the David Coleman inspired single *Quite Extraordinary* and LP *Three Football Grounds*; comic raconteur Frank Sidebottom with *The Robins Aren't Bobbins* about non-League Altrincham; The Wedding Present with their debut LP *George Best*; and The Housemartins with their LP *London 0 Hull 4*. All of these musical tributes to football were cast in the shadow of the 'first wave' of football fanzines.

4 Rebels without a clue:
Football fanzine subculture

Leisure, then, begins beyond need. The self-interest underlying forms of communal leisure is therefore not based upon neediness, but upon enthusiasm, pleasure and enjoyment. It may perhaps be more useful to talk about an enthusiast's desires than needs. For many activities, it is then only through coming together that one can fulfil certain desires, those not available to the individual acting alone (Bishop and Hoggett, *Organising Around Enthusiasms*, 1986, p.128).

The initial motivating factor behind football fanzines is enthusiasm. As the history of *WSC* has shown, this enthusiasm may develop into something else (a livelihood), or draw zeal from different criteria (the necessity of producing a monthly magazine), but the essential ingredient is still a passion for football and the desire to express opinion. The capacity to produce fanzines by the mid 80s was enhanced by the commonplace of word processors/personal computers not only within the workplace and education, but within the home. Writing with this new 'mode of information' allowed the 'ordinary' fan access into advanced printing technology. As Mark Poster suggests "computer writing is the quintessential postmodern linguistic activity" (Poster, 1990, p.128). Desk top publishing is an ideal tool for the production of fanzines. The form of the technology corresponds with the fanzine: ephemeral, instantly transformable, and evanescent.

The actual production of football fanzines can take on a particular subversive nature itself. Like their predecessors in punk, writers and editors often rely on the (mis)use of their employer's equipment.

Photocopiers and PCs, readily available in company offices, are hijacked during lunch breaks or after hours by eager fanzine writers desperate to complete the next issue in time for scheduled release. There is a blurring of the dichotomy between work and leisure. This is not only because a fanzine might be produced in the workplace, but also because of the energy that is required in a fanzine's consummation. Jeremy Seabrook in his astute study of working class leisure describes the bizarre stranglehold that activities and pastimes can have on people's lives - the following quote could easily be describing the disposition of many a fanzine editor:

> It is, they tell you, addictive. You get obsessed, it takes you over, you get hooked, it becomes a way of life, it gets out of control. This kind of expression recurs too frequently to be ignored in people's accounts of how they spend their time. It seems to be related to the need for function; the surprise with which we respond when a stranger hasn't heard of some luminary in our field of interest for a moment breaks the collusive and supportive understanding that binds us to those who share our overriding interest, our narrow specialism. These have to be elevated, given an independent significance that validates the fascination they hold for us. But the sense of not being quite in control suggests something far from the self-determination and freely chosen occupation we like to think it is: the needs which leisure activities are called upon to answer are perhaps far more profound than the words themselves suggest (Jeremy Seabrook, *The Leisure Society*, 1988, p.7).

Seabrook's insight into the contradictory nature of dichotomies such as 'work time'/'spare time' etc., is pertinent to the way in which football fanzines can take over their producers lives, especially when they are edited and produced by a single individual. The amount of time and effort that goes into producing a fanzine is usually disproportionate to its price and the amount of profit (if any) the editor(s) may receive. Moreover, it is time and effort, lack of motivation, a waning of enthusiasm and sheer frustration at not being able to gather enough material that often accounts for the disappearance of fanzines. Access to resources also plays its part, but this belies the fanaticism of many football followers who can often bring new meaning to the old adage "where there's a will there's a way". If nothing else, football fans show a large amount of perseverance and resilience (spiced with an ironic ray of hope!)

Although a handful of single club fanzines existed before the appearance of *Off The Ball* and *WSC* in 1986 - *City Gent* (Bradford City) and *Terrace Talk* (York City) were early role models for the late 80s club based fanzines - it was the two general fanzines which provided inspiration to others. By the end of 1986 there were signs that more fanzines were being produced or were in the pipeline. Mike Ticher openly enthused about new publications as *WSC* started to review new fanzines and list them at the back of the magazine. In December 1986 he wrote:

> Suffice it to say that everything that appears in this column is worth sampling. Think how much money you spend on programmes during a season, and what a huge kick you get out of them. Now think about the small amount it costs to send off for one (or all) of these (*WSC*, No. 5).

A distinctive distribution network was also beginning to take shape. Sportspages the specialist book shop in London was one of the major early outlets of fanzines, as was a similar shop in Edinburgh, Football Crazy. John Gausted of Sportspages remembers writing to *WSC* suggesting that it might be useful for the shop to stock the fanzine. After receiving the first batch of 20 copies Gausted says:

> I can recall feeling quite pleased that I had added this rather odd item to the stock, as I placed them neatly on the floor next to the football book shelves ... Despite the pressure they exert on space, our commitment to stocking them has never wavered, both for the cynical reason that we sell a lot of them and for the more worthy reason that we think they are 'a good thing'. And anyway they've been very good for us, providing both publicity and cred (*The Absolute Game*, March/April 92).

Football fanzines also tapped into a more established network of distributors, the independent record shops. Selectadisc in Nottingham was one of the first to support the sale of football fanzines. As the shops' manager Jim Cooke explained to me:

> I started selling fanzines in October/November '86. I came across

Off The Ball at a Notts County crisis meeting in September '86, bought it, loved it and it reminded me of *Foul* from my youth. I bought *Foul* from Selectadisc and as I was now manager of the shops I thought it my duty to stock it. I was a member of the FSA and realised football needed a new image and I thought by promoting *Off The Ball*, *WSC*, *Orienteer*, *City Gent* this would help.

Cooke was inspired by the growth of fanzines and decided to produce his own fanzine *The Pie*. He says:

I was fed up being classed a nutter just because my mates and I would trek off to say Norwich/Ipswich midweek to see the Notts County Youth Team. My mates and I started *The Pie* coming out January '87 and since then the "fanzine thing" has snowballed.

Selectadisc became so embroiled within the 'snowball' effect of football's alternative press that the front windows of one of its three shops became a montage of fanzine titles. Fanzines invariably detracted from the main function of the shop (as did the sale of replica football shirts and football T-shirts later on) yet the corollary of such enthusiasm was a stronger link with a section of the shop's customers. Cooke concludes:

I think as music is constantly changing and upfront, people who work in them - independent shops that is - are more aware of what a person wants at any specific time. People wanted fanzines and our shop was into it just before this so we reaped the benefit and vice versa.

Rough Trade in London was another of the independent shops to stock football fanzines from their inception. Adrian Goldberg was a regular customer of theirs and asked the shop to stock a copy of *Off The Ball*. Again by the end of the 80s the shop was stocking up to 40 titles. There was no systematic way of stocking the fanzines, either an editor would pop in with the latest copy, *Imperfect Match* (Arsenal) and *Fortunes Always Hiding* (West Ham) were regulars, or fanzines were sent through the post. This often created an administrative nightmare, not only was the shop restricted for space - especially with the growth of CD's - but unsold copies often cost more to return to the sender than the money received from the fanzine. Nevertheless, football fanzines neatly exploited the established networks of the music trade. Dave Sewell from Rough Trade contends:

> ... while there is a vacuum in music fanzine culture [partly he suggests due to the lack of "worthwhile bands"], a preexisting and vibrant soccer culture will move in and use its distribution network. It will always come down to individuals, those who produce them and the personal interests of those who stock them.

More recently another specialist football/sports shop has been opened in Nottingham called The Beautiful Game. A former PE teacher, Paul Bethell, decided to open a shop in the summer of 1992 dedicated to selling fanzines and football books in a similar vein to Sportspages of London. According to Paul;

> I keep the sort of books Smith's don't ... I see myself developing and leaning more to the literature eventually. Fanzines are very transient - in three years they might have all but disappeared (*Nottingham Evening Post*, 14.9.92).

An alternative football fan network began to emerge. Editors would send each other copies of their fanzines which would then be reviewed. Editors and writers would meet, either regionally at FSA meetings, or from all over the country at matches, either in the pub or on the terraces themselves. This flow of correspondence between editors produced a form of mutual aid among supporters. In the early years of growth there emerged an unwritten rule about not criticizing the work of other fanzines - at least not overtly - as there was a common sense of opinion that fans, no matter which club they supported, shared similar problems and similar objectives. This 'common sense' had much to do with the noises the FSA were making in the media in the wake of the 1985 tragedies and also with the possibility of a compulsory membership scheme (ID Cards) proposed by central government. Some fanzines had 'guest appearances' by writers from another fanzine. Editors would steal articles from other fanzines when their team was mentioned. For instance, *The Square Ball* (Leeds United) introduced a 'propaganda' page to cater for other fanzines remarks about *TSB* or Leeds United in general.

The sharing or, as was more often, copying of ideas was also prevalent: there emerged a *fanzine formula*. After Hillsborough there was another surge in fanzines, many produced by younger fans who took up a standard fanzine formula. Tom Davies (*WSC* No. 43) parodied "the persona of a fanzine person" in an article entitled 'Born To Be A Fanzine Writer'. He produced a five point plan to "the lifestyle and the writing technique" needed to be an editor of your own fanzine much in the way that *Sniffin' Glue* over ten years earlier had produced a three step guide to being in a punk band. With tongue in cheek Davies cut deep into the 'real' motivating factor behind the 'purpose' of joining "the cutting edge of football's late '80s/early '90s sub-culture":

> You may have read somewhere (in *The Independent* or some such publication) that fanzines are inspired by the need for a radical, dissenting, articulate voice reflecting the hopes, fears, passions and quirks of the Downtrodden Football Fan. Yeah, yeah, that may be a secondary consideration, but your main motive for getting involved is the chance to see your name in print loads of times, thereby appearing dead cool, impressing all the girls, and perhaps even getting a chance to be on the telly if someone from Channel 4 makes a documentary (*WSC*, No. 43).

There then followed the four other steps in the guide: content (including "a couple of surreal, badly drawn cartoons slagging off a rival team's fans or manager complete with allegations about sexual activities/deviation"), selling ("Now's the time to find out who your real friends are"), favourite bands ("The tried and tested method is to use the titles of obscure 12 inch B-sides as match report headlines"), and politics ("don't let any SWP or Militant members get involved in your magazine"). Although the article is a wind up there are accurate representations in this particular simulacrum of a fanzine writer, albeit a male one!

The reason why fans decide to start up a fanzine invariably revolves around the need for representation: to provide 'ordinary' fans with a voice. Various other reasons cut across this accepted desire to rail against the inadequacies of football administrators, the government and the media. Common themes appear to be: the club programme was glossy and inadequate; the club lacked a fanzine or one that was interesting; the club was facing some form of crisis either financial or on the pitch; editors were ex-pats, displaced from their clubs' home town. The following quotes give a taste of the multifarious reasons for starting a fanzine:

In the Autumn of 1989, amidst the doom and gloom of 'Pools perilous position of 92nd. in the League (with Auto-relegation to 'The Conference'), a Hartlepool United fan who was based in Colchester wrote to the Hartlepool Mail's sports editor asking if anyone was interested in starting a fanzine. 'Pools was one of the few clubs at that time without one. As I was also an ex-pat who was resident in Colchester in 1989, I immediately made contact with the letter-writer, Dave Shedden. Amazingly, he lived about 400 yards away - was this fate? Better still, several others made contact (including another chap in Colchester!) and soon, enough ideas had manifested themselves so that our 1st. issue could go on sale on Boxing-Day 1989. Dave Sheddon had previously been involved with an Ipswich Town fanzine, and was able to help with contacts for printing and layout (Greame Young, co-editor, *Monkey Business* [Hartlepool United]).

Our fanzine was started by a hardcore of five people 18 months ago in response to numerous requests for club information from supporters across the country and as a means of giving supporters a voice in what were troubled times for Berwick (little has changed as our last chairman has just done a bunk with an estimated £130,000 of club funds!). We planned the start up of the fanzine over a four month period, wrote the necessary articles, found a printer and got a loan from the supporters' club for the start up costs and away we went thankfully to success (Colin Beveridge, editor, *From The Grove To The Harrow* [Berwick Rangers]).

I was fed up of waiting for a decent Derby 'zine, and so decided to do one myself. I had graduated last summer from Sheffield Polytechnic. As employment prospects were (and still are!) minimal, it gave me an opportunity to keep the brain cells ticking over, and it meant I had something to do, instead of vegetating at home (Nick Wheat, editor, *C-Stander* [Derby County]).

We were on a J & P training course for one year. We asked 'could

59

we put a 'zine together?'. The job placement agency was very helpful and let us tear away. We then worked away and got issue 1 out in about 4 weeks. It sold very well. We were able to pay off all our debts and even make a small profit. Because our course lasts only one year, we thought 'right we'll do the fanzine for one season while were on the course' (Speed, editor, *The One And Only* [General]).

Fanzine titles and their origins provide yet another reason for the explosion of the alternative football publications. Moreover, it is the title of the fanzine which has produced most of the phenomenon's humour, their irony and inventiveness providing the staple diet upon which the success of these publications rests. Football has developed its own language or vocabulary - most of it enshrined in football commentator parlance - which has been plundered to death by editors eager to find a catchy, humorous title for their fanzine. From the commentary box there is *And Smith Must Score* (Brighton and Hove Albion) parodying the knack of commentators to provide the kiss of death to goal scoring opportunities; from the terraces is *Sing When We're Fishing/Ploughin'* (Grimsby Town/Norwich City) a variation on a standard terrace retort and *Come On Dagenham Use Your Forwards* (Dagenham); from armchair supporters there is *Liverpool Are On The Telly Again* (Norwich City) or because of this fact *When Sunday Comes* (Liverpool); from nicknames there is *Flashing Blade* (Sheffield United) and *Relient Robin* (Wrexham); from the players there is *A Load Of Bull* (Wolves) referring to Steve Bull; from parts of the ground their is *King Of The Kippax* (Manchester City) and *C-Stander* (Derby County) which editor Nick Wheat argues "is the only seated area for home fans that generates any atmosphere and can take care of intruders without police assistance"; or from street names near the ground *Walking Down The Halbeath Road* (Dunfermline Athletic). Other fanzines draw on local colloquialisms or something peculiar to their region: *Talk Of The Toon* (Newcastle United), *Grorty Dick* (West Bromwich Albion) which is a Black Country delicacy and *Mi Whippets Dead* (Rotherham United). Many other fanzines find their inspiration from other realms of popular culture, mainly film or music: *The Occasional Terrorist* (Tooting and Mitcham fans), *A Nightmare On Dee Street* (Glentoran) and *Dial M For Merthyr* (Merthyr Tydfil) or *World Shut Your Mouth!* (Rangers) from the song with the same title by Julian Cope and *My Eyes Have Seen The Glory* (Spurs) from a line in The Smiths track *These Things Take Time*. But perhaps the most intriguing titles come from those without any apparent reference point or meaning whatsoever. Among these more surrealist titles which can only be fathomed out by those who produce them are: *The Gibbering Clairvoyant* (Dumbarton), *Tomato Soup And Lentils* (Leeds United and Arbroath), *Psycho Arab* (Dundee United) and *Monkey Business* (Hartlepool United) which according to its editor Greame Young "refers to a Hartlepool legend involving a French spy (The Monkey) and a visit to the hangman's gallows!".

Many of these bizarre titles pay homage to club traditions or obscure football anecdotes which communicate a unique bond with the fans of a particular club. All fanzine titles - and indeed their contents - allude to some part of the football ritual, which makes symbolic communication possible. Invariably, fanzines rely upon comic transgressions of dominant values and ideas on football from both fans and wider society. Equally, the tragic discourses of the football ritual are also employed to capture the essence of football fandom: *Mission Impossible* (Darlington FC) and *Mission Terminated* (Torquay United) are apt illustrations of fanzines using the painful emotional moments of the game (in these cases the unlikelihood of success) as a form of tragic comment.

Recourse to other football traditions came in the guise of the reincarnation of the football writers use of the pseudonym. As commented earlier in Chapter 2, in the embryonic stages of football journalism, many columns were written under a pseudonym. 'Mad Mac' of *The Absolute Game* (Scottish General) and North Bank Norman of *Fortunes Always Hiding* (West Ham Utd.) are two of the best known contemporary exponents, there are hundreds more. The use of a pseudonym not only keeps the writer's anonymity, but helps create a mystique, which lends a certain 'underground' feeling to the fanzine - something which many fanzine contributors believe is central to 'fanzine ethics'. Such ethics are not fixed and have shifted over time. Mutual agreement not to overly criticize other fanzines, to work outside the mainstream media, to have independence from the clubs and promote positive forms of fan politics appear to be the early conceptions of what fanzines ought to be.

A survey of the fanzine list in *WSC* from the mid 80s to the 90s gives a good impression of just how fast fanzine culture took hold of the supporters imagination. In January 1988 there were 22, in January

1989 there were 215, in January 1990 the list was so extensive it was temporarily split into three sections over three issues, and finally, by January 1992 there were well over 600 titles that had come and gone. The ephemeral nature of fanzines makes any definitive listing and title count almost impossible. Every month *WSC* can list over ten new titles, with as many becoming defunct.

Yet from 1987 to the end of 1990 fanzines grew at a phenomenal rate. This explosion attracted extensive publicity. The *Observer Magazine* (19/4/87) provided a tongue in cheek review of fanzines, courtesy of Roy Race. With the heading 'Write Stuff For The Fans' this pastiche of the Melchester Rovers 'player manager' suggested:

> Fanzines are to soccer what Jimmy Hill is to 'Match Of The Day':
> some say indispensable, others say surplus to requirements.

This early testament to the rise of fanzines was later to be followed by the NME's guide to fanzines and how to produce one in May 1989 in which Richard North reemphasized the incredible momentum of the fanzine boom:

> If the fanzines' eruption is old news, then the scope and intensity
> of its continuation is a surprise. Rather than tailing off or dying,
> as some rashly predicted, there are five or six new 'zines
> appearing every week.

Along with a review of Dunning et al's *The Roots Of Football Hooliganism* in 1988, the *Young Guardian* slipped in a small article on two brothers Carl and Howard Prosser who edited *The Lions Roar* (Milwall) and *In The Loft* (QPR) respectively. Alongside a photograph of Howard proudly plugging his wares outside QPR, the article ran:

> The influence of the fanzines is now farspread. Some managers
> and players have started replying to the points in the fanzines and
> the fans are always ready to send in their views. Carl even
> showed me a letter from Tokyo by a Japanese Milwall fan.

Anecdotes of this kind are not unfamiliar to many fanzine editors who receive letters from fellow fans from all over the world. However, it is the relationship closer to home - with the club itself -

which is far more intriguing. A club fanzine's number one enemy is often the Chairman and the board of directors. This may still apply even if the team are doing well. A prime target was the late Robert Maxwell who showed little empathy for the clubs he was involved in (Oxford United, Derby County, and a tampering with Spurs). Maxwell's dealings in football were received with the utmost suspicion by the majority of fans, the subsequent uncovering of his fraudulent commercial investments provides adequate evidence for such concern.

Maxwell's interest in Spurs was an issue raised in one of the few investigative accounts of a football club's behind the scenes melodrama in the 1990s. *Heroes And Villains* by Alex Fynn and Lynton Guest (1991) attempted to tell "The inside story of the 1990/91 season at Arsenal and Tottenham Hotspur". However, their approach - from a PR/marketing background - fails to capture the surreptitious nature of football club life, in a way that fanzines through intense, investigative work, have unearthed the broader meanings of such wrangles for the majority of fans. The investigative work of fanzines is undertaken with the opinion that fans have a vested interest in the club, which is increasingly being denied them because of various economic imperatives the club feels are more important.

Not surprisingly, some fanzines have had to face the wrath of club directors and officials for 'overstepping the mark'. Football fans have grown accustomed to being highly policed in and around football grounds but surveillance was taken to new heights when editors began to be moved on while selling their publications outside grounds, or were banned from the ground altogether by the club. In September 1990 the legal regulation of fanzines reached a profound level when *Gulls Eye* from Brighton and Hove Albion supporters was accused of libel by the club director John Campbell. Ian Hart and Peter Kennard the co-editors of the *Eye* reached an out of court settlement with the club, which amounted to an apology for an offensive article written by Attila the Stockbroker and the payment of the club's legal costs of £6000. Such extreme measures which attempt to silence the fanzine merely accentuates the division between those who administer football and the fans. A *Gulls Eye* Fighting Fund was set up to assist the payment incurred by the editors, one of whom was unemployed. Ray Chuter, a Brighton fan based in Manchester set up a fanzine called *Pretty In Pink* and produced a T-shirt in aid of the fund, and Attila the Stockbroker wrote an article in *WSC* in which he argued:

> *Gulls Eye* is caustic, passionate and occasionally way over the top, but its editors have spoken out in a way which has certainly struck a chord with the fans (average sales are currently around 2000 per issue). It is without doubt a thorn in the side of the board, and this ridiculous libel action is a clear attempt to intimidate it out of existence (*WSC*, No. 48).

Despite this particularly vindictive attack on the fans' attempt to voice their opinion, the majority of the independent publications are tolerated. A proportion of fanzines have gained a certain amount of respectability or at least acknowledgement from football clubs. Manchester City souvenir shop, like others across the country, sells a selection of fanzines. City actually approached *Blueprint*, the most popular City fanzine, to document the 1991/92 season on video, recording the fans at Maine Road as the season unfolded. Moreover, there are instances of fanzines donating money to the clubs they support. For instance, co-operation on this level is not uncommon among fanzines of non-league clubs. As John Gray editor of Basingstoke's fanzines *Get Lawrence On* describes:

> Every penny which is raised is put straight back into the club. With the Chairman owning club sponsors The Basingstoke Press, we have now found the ideal arrangement. He prints the fanzines (well copies them) for nothing thus the 50p price means 50p for the club.

As Rogan Taylor's history of supporters' organizations has shown, this benevolent nature of fans has pervaded the game from its early professional beginnings. Yet, Non-League football has quite distinct qualities in the way clubs are controlled compared to their professional counterparts. Martin Lacey has suggested that the access with which the smaller, non-league football club function is part of the reason for an upsurge of interest in these small town clubs plus, he suggests, the football is far more entertaining.

Why some fanzine editors entertain involvement and co-operation while others go out of their way to maintain critical independence is a fundamental question when discerning how fans relate to the club they support. Editors have to balance their enthusiasm for football and their passion for the team they support, with the sharp criticism and inventive wit their readers become accustomed to. So often fanzines, disappear or disappoint because of their lack of ideas or aggressive vitriol. An example of controversy over defining the role of fanzines occurred when Millwall's *No One Likes Us* sponsored a League fixture against Plymouth Argyle for £1,750 in February 1991, with money raised through the sale of their publication. Milwall had pioneered the Football In The Community Schemes and although initially wary of the fanzine's proposal, Reg Burr the chairman, warmed to the idea. George Craig a contributor to the fanzine was reported as saying:

> The fact that the Milwall board have agreed to the sponsorship, despite our viciously satirical editorials, shows how they have a sense of humour (*The Guardian*, 14.2.92).

Another Milwall publication *Someone Likes Us* did object to their 'rivals' tactics of sponsorship, building on a certain amount of animosity which had grown out of an article by Craig which falsely linked *Someone Likes Us* to the National Front. Reports of violent threats over the telephone ensued and the police were called in to investigate. Such rivalries between fanzine editors who support the same team are increasingly widespread. The majority are humorous struggles over quality of content and quantity of sales, but some are fought with an intensity which belies the ideals with which fanzines were associated in the mid 80s. Other developments which appeared to run conversely to the early conceptions of the fanzine involved the movement from crude to glossy presentation. *The Spur* (Tottenham Hotspur) and *The Gooner* (Arsenal) became two immaculately produced magazines, the former inflating its price over £2.00.

The principles of fanzines began to be debated among the 'alternative football fraternity' in FSA meetings and at one particular event called 'You'll Never Walk Alone' during the Readers and Writers week at the Midlands Art Centre in April 1991. The panel, chaired by Adrian Goldberg, included John Duncan from *WSC*, David Worton from *A Load Of Bull* (Wolverhampton Wanderers) and Simon Wright from *Grorty Dick* (West Bromwich Albion). The debate entitled 'Fanzines: Fight or Fall?' wrestled with the growth of a perceived turmoil among the producers of fanzines. The panel, and the audience which was made up of a high proportion of fanzine editors themselves, reached common opinion that if fanzines had a future, there was a need for a sense of responsibility. However, such a sanctimonious outlook could also be perceived as betraying the vitriolic reverence fanzines can have for the way football is managed.

Similar debates about the past achievements and future potential of fanzines have been addressed within fanzines themselves. The 5th. anniversary issue of *The Absolute Game* (Mar/April 1992) asked "Fanzines, still a vital outlet for the concerns of supporters or well past their sell-by date?" Craig Young of *No Idle Talk* and *Scottish Zine Scene* lamented the passing of some of his favourite publications and stated:

> What you have to remember is that with the exception of an elite half-dozen, fanzine editorial teams consist of about two people. One person owns the computer or typewriter, writes half the articles and basically runs the show. The other person will be a major contributor. After that, nearly all fanzines rely on contributions from their readers. I've lost count of the amount of letters I've had from editors who complain about lack of contributions and time to write articles themselves (*TAG*, March/April 92).

To overcome the difficulties of one individual single-handedly putting together a fanzine, compounded by the unreliability of contributors, some fanzines have been established as going concerns. Other fanzines have attempted to survive as going concerns, providing a livelihood for its contributors. For example, *The Square Ball* (Leeds United) was originally set up by a Manchester United fan, Alex Griffiths, who had previously been involved in the production of *The Shankill Skinhead* (Manchester United). The title of the Leeds fanzine was as a "piss take" of the Revie era and was targeted to cater for a large audience which had not successfully been exploited by the other Leeds fanzines *Marching On Together* and *The Hanging Sheep*. *TSB* was glossy, expensive (£1), printed by Snowshine Ltd. - which also produced *What's On*, a guide to cultural activities in Leeds - and soon found its way into many Leeds newsagents. Griffiths left the magazine after a handful of issues to concentrate on a career in journalism back in Manchester, but TSB continued to go from strength to strength, building on the upturn in the fortunes of Leeds United. The company also went on to produce the fanzines *The Magic Sponge* and *Tackler,* both aimed at a national audience. In an attempt to maintain popularity or broaden horizons, several fanzines have diversified their activities by merchandising products related to their publication or the club they support. Transgressing into other forms of popular cultural production, such as music and fashion, these enterprising initiatives draw upon and feed into a common 'alternative' culture which has its roots in punk and was nurtured by the 'indie' scene of the 1980s. The tradition of producing free flexi-discs with punk and music fanzines has been esoterically re-established by football's alternative press. 'Blue Moon' which had been adopted by Manchester City fans was re-interpreted and re-mixed with the sound of the terraces by DJ/producer Adrian Sherwood of On-U-Sounds and brought out as a flexi-disc with the fanzine *Blueprint* (Issue 15). *The Spur* (Tottenham Hotspur), in celebration of their club's return to Europe and in opposition to the fanzine crisis the club were enduring in 1991, produced a 48 page edition with a Cup Winners Supplement and a free flex-disc featuring, among others, members of Lush and The Cocteau Twins, at the bumped up price of £2.95. Other excursions into vinyl came from *Beyond The Boundary* (Oldham Athletic) who produced the 7" single 'The Roger Rap' with proceeds going to the player Roger Palmer's testimonial fund. *Fly Me To The Moon* (Middlesbrough) who in conjunction with the group Shrug produced a three track EP entitled *Mission From Todd* which delighted in the skills of Middlesbrough's centre-half Tony Mowbrey (now at Celtic) whose post match analysis consisted of being 'over the moon', which as the track 'Return Mission' suggests is "the ultimate in altitude training". Another fanzine *D Pleated* (Luton Town, the title a pun on their ex-manager David Pleat) produced a 7" single for "trendy young beatniks", while the inflatables craze of the late 80s inspired a collection of artists to record the LP 'Bananas' produced by *Rodney Rodney*. Finally, the endlessly banal array of recordings made by football clubs and their fans were lovingly captured on the LP *Flair 1989: The Other World of British football* produced by Confection Records. The production of records by football fanzines exemplifies the indelible links between football and music consumption. These ties, predominantly masculine, have much to do with the demographics of contemporary consumer culture. Those born in the

1960s 'baby boom' are now part of the 'post-generation' which tasted the end of the post-war growth years as children and grew up as part of the TV age while being subjected to recession and the dismantling of the welfare state. This, in part, explains the pastiche and parody of late 60s and early 70s popular culture by football fanzines youth culture in general (from long sideburns to long perms, from flared trousers to tank tops and from Thunderbirds to Scooby Doo). *Blueprint* (Manchester City) exploited this nostalgic urge by merchandising a long-sleeved shirt with the inscription 'Better Than Best' below a picture of the epitome of late 60s/early 70s 'flair' footballing talent Rodney Marsh - a statement later subverted by rival Manchester United fans who purchased the T-shirts merely to inscribe "Was He Fuck" in thick black marker pen across the back.

The most successful attempt to tap the nostalgia for 60s and 70s football has been Arkwright's replica football shirts produced by Leisureco Ltd in Leeds. To a large extent the popularity of these replica kits is of the football industry's own making. Each season clubs unveil their latest strip, costing an inordinate amount of money, with monstrous designs which seemingly get worse year after year (take for example Arsenal's 'bruised banana' away kit). Through simplicity and plainness (100% cotton in small, medium or dart player size) and shrewd marketing which uses the names of famous players to evoke a sense of authenticity ('wicked 50s shorts' as worn by Lawton and Matthews, 60s fleecy tracksuits as worn by Alf Ramsey, and 70s shirts as worn by Bremner, Best, and Bell) Leisureco has transformed itself from a cottage industry selling a small selection of kits by mail order through fanzines (originally the white Leeds kit in *TSB*) to supplying record shops and department stores with an extensive range of UK, European and international team colours. As part of the football renaissance in the UK, the company has carved a niche in the highly competitive world of sports manufacturing, its alternative form of 'enterprise culture', exploiting the disillusion many fans feel with the synthetic replica shirts on sale in high-street sports shops, manufactured by multi-national corporations like Adidas, Puma or Umbro.

5 Vanguard or vagabond?
A history of *When Saturday Comes*

The 5th birthday and 50th edition of *When Saturday Comes* (not a fanzine but 'The Half Decent Football Magazine' as it prefers to call itself) provided an opportunity for reflection both serious (by the 'quality' press) and the tongue-in-cheek (by itself). The current editor Andy Lyons instead of a 'self-indulgent trawl' through back issues gave a satirical account of "The True (?) Story of *WSC* " entitled "When Saturday Came". He confessed:

> WSC began as a twelve page supplement to *Cardigan,* a short-lived magazine aimed at the thousands of middle-aged men who rediscover childhood hobbies once their marriages have ground to a standstill (*WSC,* No. 50).

In the 'quality' press Dave Hill in *The Independent on Sunday* (7 April 1991) described the magazine as "The half-decent defender of those long-suffering supporters" and "the exemplar of a phenomenon". Simon Barnes in *The Times* (10 April 1991) suggested that:

> WSC has not gone legit: not in any establishment-loving sense. This is a fanzine that has grown up and lost its pimples and started to shave.

To celebrate the magazine's transition from stapled photocopied sheets to a finely produced and well distributed football monthly a party was held at The Rocket, London, with guest DJ Adrian Sherwood (producer of the classic football record Barmy Army *The English Disease*). What is important about these anniversary celebrations is that they stem from a football fan organizing around an enthusiasm, without any prior knowledge of writing about football and with no conception of making a living out of doing so. In what he termed as 'Surely Emotional Farewell of the Season?' Mike Ticher (founder of *WSC* and beleaguered Chelsea fan who loved to hate Ken Bates) gave a brief and nostalgic look back to the beginning of his fanzine:

> When *WSC* first started, equipped only with a wobbly typewriter and a lovingly-nurtured sense of outrage, it was inconceivable to us that so many other people would share our frustration at the way football was run, and written about. It's inevitably been a slow process establishing contact with those people, but the realisation from the start that we weren't just isolated eccentrics is the one reason why the magazine is still here two years, against all the odds (*WSC*, No. 18).

From its 'bedsit origins' in March 1986, the first issue of 200 copies had twelve pages and cost 15p, the magazine (as its editors have always preferred to call it) has a readership approaching 40,000. When the magazine began Ticher and Lyons were working in a record shop, and at the time of Ticher's emigration to Australia in the summer of 1988 they each received an allowance of approximately £40 per week. By this time they had recruited student Bill Brewster (avid Grimsby Town fan) after advertising for someone to help out during the day. By the 89/90 season, after the publication of their first book, the 96 page *Offside*, they tried to get the magazine on a more permanent footing, paying each other £300 a month. This gradually increased until quite recently when they joined PAYE as fully fledged employees of *WSC*. There are now eight employees either full or part-time. Apart from the magazines and the books (of which there are now three) *WSC* indulged in commercial spinoffs such as T-shirts. But the editors were conscious of not making a lot of money out of the name of the magazine, keeping *WSC* merchandise within reasonable limits, not wanting to appear too commercial, and as something that would not detract from people's interest in the game itself. Lyons gives his reasons for such fears:

> The only problem with making a bit more money out of the magazine, in theory, the more stuff we do the more people we

need to work a bit more and there is a chance that we might get a bit more remote from our readers.

Such an attitude, of maintaining a small-scale staff and managing the conflict between progress and principle, reflects the wider principles of the intelligent football lobby with which the magazine openly identifies. But the tensions between the modernization of the game and football nostalgia is also mirrored in *WSC*'s resistance to change, which to Dave Hill:

> Sometimes seems inspired by a kind of aesthetic conservatism as well as a dislike of being steam-rollered by power brokers. This can lead the magazine, fleetingly, into the same camp as those they most dislike: that Bates fellow for instance (*Independent on Sunday*, 7.4.91).

The economic potential of the magazine has been recognized by none other than the editors of *Viz* who launched a takeover bid, with the promise of a circulation up to 150,000 a month. But *Viz* to Lyons and his co-editors is the very antithesis of what *WSC* is all about. By July 1989 the first musings of taking on advertisements were mentioned. But it was not until April 1990 (*WSC*, No. 38) that adverts were introduced. Lyons explains the difficulties over this issue:

> With advertising we'd been holding off for a couple of years. It basically paid, and brought in enough money to pay somebody's wages. It was quite a big thing to do. We'd been mentioning it for a while about advertising and I think we thought it was the way we should go and nobody really complained about it. We were concerned about the idea, but decided we needed to do it as long as the adverts were tied in with the outlook of the magazine. We weren't going to take adverts for South African airlines for instance.

The rise of *WSC* from its makeshift beginnings to the shelves of major newsagents can be likened to other magazine subcultures which organized around enthusiasms and leisure practices. For instance, *Hot Rod Magazine* in the US and the numerous scooter magazines in Britain over the last thirty years. Similarly, these magazines played a pivotal role in their subcultures. Moorehouse

(1984) suggests that such specialist magazines have a two-fold significance: they organize demand by telling people what they wanted to know, arranging matters so that the pastime was available to them; and they presented the sport/pastime to a wider constituency of readers who were not active in the subculture, but felt some affinity to the pursuit. Hence, the effect of *Hot Rod Magazine* was to change 'hot rodding' from a casual pastime into a participant and spectator sport, 'drag racing'. *WSC* to a certain degree follows this theory in the way that it has captured a new audience that was hitherto unrecognized amongst the football milieu that were fed up with what Ticher called 'cliched, hackneyed, lazy journalism' (*WSC*, No. 1) and later helped the cause of the Football Supporters Association as it campaigned against the ills of the game. However, it was with its fanzine counterparts *Off The Ball* and *The Absolute Game* , that *WSC* made its greatest impact on British football culture. By listing the names, addresses, and price (and occasional review) of many of the club based fanzines, *WSC* kick started the blossoming of a whole new phenomenon. They began to list sales outlets which were invariably record shops or specialist bookshops. As Redhead has commented on the habit of listing:

> It has proved to be a successful format for building an alternative local cultural network in an age dominated by hi-tech global media (Redhead, 1991, p.53).

As new fanzines continually emerge they are subsequently listed amongst an update which also includes fanzines which are defunct, changing name or address. John Robinson editor of *The Best of the Football Fanzines* also praised the three aforementioned fanzines:

> It was these three which were to prove the most influential in inspiring the wide range of contemporaries now available in a way that *Foul* for all it's relative success, strangely, never did (1989, p.2).

And in the *NME* (27 May 1989) an article on fanzines argued: "In the same way that the best pop fanzines make you want to go to gigs, *WSC* will have you returning to the terraces." It is the magazines attempt to maintain a balance between humour and serious comment about contemporary happenings that has ensured its survival. After the inaugural issues, where the magazines in Lyons words "got a lot off its chest", the magazines settled down into a familiar format with the emblem of a crusading footballer of 'The People' as its masthead. Although the magazine relied (and still does) on outside contributors, the 'in house' writers showed considerable journalistic flair. John Duncan, who joined the magazine as a co-editor just before Ticher departed, took care of the business side of things, and later moved on to be a full-time freelance football journalist with *The Observer* and *The Guardian*. However, although Lyons has written a column for a US magazine on the topic of European football, he has never been interested in using his experience at *WSC* as a springboard into football journalism. He was happy to co-exist alongside the mainstream media, not particularly interested in writing match reports.

In February 1990 (*WSC*, No. 36), the magazine carried out a survey of its readers, to try and establish who their readers were, and what they liked or disliked about the magazine. Questions attempting to ascertain where, when and how often readers bought the magazine were accompanied by questions designed to find out what other literature (magazines/newspapers) fans bought, and how they would like to see the magazine improved. The survey found that from a sample of 949 (they eventually received over 2000 replies) nineteen per cent claimed going to between 20-49 games. Eighty per cent watched from the terraces. The majority of the sample suggested they were happy with the magazine, but wanted it "to edge away slightly from soft focus nostalgia towards a more hard hitting, investigative stance" (*WSC*, No. 39). Andy Lyons sets out who he believes the magazine is aimed at:

> ... the average reader is probably someone in their 20's maybe ex-student, or quite likely to be a student, and the *Guardian/Independent* reader .... Someone that grew up watching football late sixties/early seventies. Predominantly male. We have got some women readers, but not that many really. But in a way there's not a great deal you can do about that. Probably not that many readers over fifty. Probably not that many under sixteen. An adult readership .... We only ever really thought about stuff that we find interesting ourselves, if other people are interested then fair enough.

The majority of nostalgic articles now tend to appear in the books which act as a repository of unpublished material. The magazine still relies on its readers to send in articles and as the readership has grown, so the magazine has developed a wide network of contacts that it can draw upon. For instance, many English fans now living in other countries regularly keep the magazine apace with the goings on around Europe and the world game in general. So in many respects the magazine although employing full-time staff acts as a forum for other people's views, pretty much how the magazine was envisaged as being from the beginning. The magazine only publishes ten per cent of the articles sent in but boasts four pages of letters. Articles that are offensive, either racist, sexist or of a sectarian type, are immediately dismissed. Slanderous local rivalry is considered by the magazine to be contrary to the original idea of the football fanzine, which was that partisanship was acceptable as long as an article that expressed such views was constructive or had something positive to say about the game in general. Lyons argues that many of the newer breed of fanzines are produced by people who merely wish to impress their friends. He considers standards to be dropping, mainly due to the number of teenagers producing fanzines who do not know enough about their own clubs.

This selective, almost moralistic viewpoint to the standards of certain fanzines came to a head in the magazines 50th edition. Following a recent debate on the letters page about fanzines, the magazine carried an article under the heading 'Out of Print' which aimed to highlight what it called a "disturbing trend". The article drew upon a letter from the father of a Liverpool fan who had copies of the Manchester United fanzine *Red Issue* and was "extremely depressed and angered" at the contents of the fanzine. Citing other fanzines such as *The Square Ball* (Leeds United) and *Mi Whippets Dead* (Rotherham United) as other examples of poor taste the article (which remained anonymous) argued that:

Two years ago, most fanzines appeared to be fighting the same battles, and railing against the same people. Clearly that is no longer the case. There was always a danger that the broadly accepted principles underpinning fanzines could be abused by people publishing magazines that openly peddle prejudice. The hope is that such filth columnists will be exposed for what they are (*WSC*, No. 50).

The article suggested that *WSC* was not in favour of censorship but could not condone blatantly offensive material. *Red Issue* was removed from the *WSC* listings, forthwith. Lyons gives his reasons as follows:

> *Red Issue* is just like the *Sun* I suppose .... But there was stuff in there we just thought was crap. It wasn't enough to ignore it. If people want to buy it OK, but we don't want to be associated with it. From his point of view he is a football fan, and he's got that right to express his views. But it seems to me that he's actually maintaining stereotypes. Like going on about Liverpool being thieves all the time, which people believe that is that kind of stuff that goes on. I just thought they've really not got anything to say.

Both the article "Out of Print" and the dropping of *Red Issue* from the listings prompted several complaints and also an apology. The apology came from *The Square Ball* for making homophobic remarks and suggested they were looking to "improve and develop" their content at all times. However, T. O. Walker a Manchester United fan argued that there are two sides to the rivalry between United and Liverpool. Referring to chants about 'Munich 58' and 'Hillsborough 89' he commented:

> Perhaps your correspondent would be well advised to look up the word 'provocation' in his dictionary. I for one am certainly fed up with the pusillanimous attitude shown by many of the people who discovered that in April 1989 cheap football disaster jokes had become a double-edged sword (*WSC*, No. 51).

The most vociferous retort came from *Red Issue* themselves who carried a cartoon of *WSC* (in the words of *Red Issue* 'Whinge, Slag and Criticise: The Half Interesting Football Mag') which was billed as being:

> As hard-hitting as Gary 'Fair Play' Lineker,
> As controversial as the United Review,
> As dull as Don Howe's Arsenal,
> For everything you need to know about football in Swaziland.

Suggesting that *WSC* was the "Mary Whitehouse of the fanzine world" and that it was "hypocritical", "sanctimonious" and "self-righteous" the fanzine argued that:

> By not advertising our address they are denying their readership a chance to buy *Red Issue* and form their own opinions. Instead, they're more than happy to let people read their views with the attitude, 'What we say must be right, you don't need to read *Red Issue* to see if what we say is correct.

This iconoclastic view of *WSC*'s idiosyncrasies reflects a growing feeling among certain fanzine writers that the 'half decent football magazine' is becoming too respectable. However, *WSC*'s movement into the mainstream of football publications reflects a broader shift in the respectability of football fanzines in general. Fanzines have established themselves as a vital source of information not only to fans but to the media. Herein lies another major success of *WSC* in helping to persuade the football press, and to a certain extent society as a whole, that all fans are not hooligans. Several mainstream football writers have been keen on promoting fanzines: Patrick Barclay and Phil Shaw of *The Independent* for instance. However, there is a certain antagonism to fanzines, partly due to a generation gap between those who write fanzines and those at the top of the football journalist profession. People like Brian Glanville of *The Times* for instance, has been dismissive of fanzines, defending his 'professional' credentials to be a football journalist. Yet, this does not seem to bother Lyons who argues that *WSC* is quite happy to co-exist alongside figures such as Glanville, believing the magazines approach to be valid in its own right.

Finally, the magazine has made excursions into television, sometimes used as alternative football fan ambassadors of the game, or in the case of BBC 2's *Standing Room Only* taking a consultants role in advising the programmes producers of ideas of who to contact. But Lyons is sceptical of the BBC's attempt to simulate the fanzine on television, believing that the humour does not come across, and seems a bit smug. It is clear that Lyons does not want the magazine to broaden its horizons too far, allowing himself and his co-editors to keep in control of their livelihood. Moreover, this is made even more evident from this final quote:

We're not desperate to get into TV. We might get some money but we quite like doing what we do, we don't like say "this is a means of stepping into the media" particularly. A bloke from the Labour Party affiliated newspaper *The Socialist* did an interview a couple of weeks ago and he asked us a lot of stuff about what's behind our magazine, what's our agenda and all this kind of stuff. And we really haven't got one. I think once you start to step back from the magazine and analyse what you're trying to do with it, who is reading it, all that kind of stuff you just go round in circles, you know. You just end up doing nothing. We never really think of any concise way of what we do. It's like we drifted into it as a full time job. It's a ridiculous, absurd job really, it's quite a silly sort of thing for an adult to do. But at the same time we might as well do it, for the simple reason that I enjoy football.

With a stable circulation approaching 40,000 per month *WSC* appears to have found a comfortable niche within the genre of football magazines that specifically address a market for men. Much of this success can be attributed to a blend of features and articles that resonate with its readership. Despite its transformation from photocopied sheets to glossy exterior, the magazine continues to appeal to its readers footballing sensibilities. This affective alliance between fanzine writer and reader builds upon a new subjectivity in sports writing hitherto lacking, or possibly censored, within the previous discursive field of sports journalism. Sports discourse, like any discourse, is:

> ... constituted by the difference between what one could say correctly at one period (under the rules of grammar and logic) and what is actually said. The discursive field is, at a specific moment the law of this difference (Foucault, 1991, p.63).

WSC has been central, along with the plethora of club fanzines, in transforming this discursive field.

WSC's position within sports journalism's discursive field can be illustrated by using David Rowe's (1992) analysis of four 'modes of sports writing' typified as: 'hard news', 'soft news', 'orthodox rhetoric' and 'reflexive analysis'. Each of these modes, Rowe argues:

> ... operate to cover sport, to position sport in the cultural and

social structure and to negotiate the splits between participant and spectator, partisanship and impartiality, and ... between writer and reader.

In regard to football journalism 'hard news' consists of sober treatments on transfers, injuries and match reports mirroring the more traditional forms of news reporting. 'Soft news' is entertainment orientated, focussing on celebrities of the game and deploying hackneyed football cliches, self-conscious humour and ghosted narratives more akin to the gossip columns of film, television and popular music magazines than the sobriety of 'hard news' items. 'Orthodox rhetoric' is a mode of sports writing which 'adopts a form of advocacy or editorial journalism instead of reportage.' This form of sports discourse, which stimulates debate by adopting the position of an interest group or sports philosophy, was particularly prominent in the aftermath of the Bradford, Heysel, and Hillsborough tragedies and over issues of the legal regulation of the football industry. Finally, 'reflexive analysis' addresses the phenomenology of sport discourse itself and, as Rowe suggests:

> ... recognises not only its own function in the representation of sport but also the tension between universalism [an abstract ideal] and particularism [the lived experience] in sport (ibid, p.106).

WSC clearly embodies the latter two modes of sports writing rather than the former. As witnessed above by the interview with the magazine's editor, Andy Lyons, WSC is socially and culturally representative of its readership despite the occasional run in with dissenting voices from within the fanzine community itself. The magazine eschews any formal style of match reporting, typified by the mode of 'hard news', but may include features which are reminiscent of 'eye witness' reports whose focus is not so much on the action on the field, as with the wider experience of being a football fan going to a match. WSC humour invariably parodies the mode of 'soft sports news' (itself a conscious parody of football melodrama) resulting in surreal cartoons or hilarious skits which offer a symbolic gesture of contempt for this particular mode of sports writing. Even photo-journalism does not escape, immediately evident from the back catalogue of WSC front covers which combine the use of bubble captions and witty headlines to lampoon photograph's of players, managers, officials and politicians alike (in the style of *Private Eye*).

Rowe (1992) further argued that the existence of fanzines has created a 'two-tiered sports literary structure' not dissimilar to divisions in other media forms (film, music, and radio) between 'cottage industries' and commercial media organizations. While this may be true in terms of the relationship between the myriad club fanzines and the popular press, *WSC* occupies a different position, which appears to combine three strategies: independence (in terms of ownership and editorial freedom); partisanship, not with a particular team but with readers, fanzine writers and football fans in general; and partnership, with commercial organizations (in terms of merchandising, foreign excursions and publishing). This final, and most recent step, partnership with commercial publishers, is a most significant development in the magazine's history. The publications *My Favourite Year* (1993) and *Shot* (1994) both bear the sensibility and aesthetic judgment of taste of *WSC*. The first is a collection of essays by the 'new' football writers on a particularly memorable year in the history of the club they support, the latter, a romantic photographic homage to the icons of seventies football. Both books were conceived by *WSC* staff with the involvement of prominent figures in sports journalism, Nick Hornby (writer/editor) and Eamonn McCabe (sports photographer). *My Favourite Year* and *Shot!* were both published by H. F. & G. Witherby an imprint of the publishing group Cassell plc, once owned by CBS Publishing, and now, after regaining its independence in 1986 has an annual turnover in excess of £14 million.

It cannot be denied that were it not for the pioneering work of *WSC*, and the mushrooming of fanzines that followed, that this new sub-genre of football book would not be published. However, it also emphasizes the adaptability of the multinational commercial media to exploit new markets which hitherto had not been accommodated and inadvertently encouraged an 'independent' formation of cultural production and consumption. From its meagre and innocent beginning in March 1986, *WSC* is now a symbolic trade mark, its logo a signifier of quality to eager consumers of football ephemera.

6　Are you sitting comfortably? Politics, supporters organizations and fanzines

Heysel Stadium: It's easy to remember
How the game continued despite the disaster
'With all those millions of viewers, we've got to carry on
It would be financial suicide to stop at this point'

And there's a ready made scapegoat, ready to blame
Hooligans fighting, ruining the game
Ignoring the bad planning and cramming in of fans
Right next to each other on crumbling stands

Putting money before safety caused those deaths
Whilst greedy bosses in their boxes shout and turn red:
'Get those bodies back the full ten yards!
They're covering up the advertising boards'
(Sportchestra, *101 Songs About Sport*).

ID Cards? Bananas!

The tragic events in 1985 augured a new moment in the politics of British football. The 'opium of the people' has traditionally been associated with the psephology of the Labour Party and socialist politicians were more likely to use footballing metaphors in their campaign speeches than their Tory counterparts. However, for many people in the game, football and politics do not mix. This constricted, at times myopic viewpoint was shattered indefinitely during the mid 80s. Political 'concern' about the game was augmented by Mrs

Thatcher when she declared 'something must be done!' after witnessing torn up plastic seats flying across the pitch in a full blooded scrap between Luton and Millwall fans on television.

Violent deaths at Birmingham and Heysel, plus the horrific fatalities caused by the combustible terracing at Valley Parade heightened the Government's concern. Persisting with the theory that 'football hooliganism' (never clearly defined) was the root of 'the problem', a whole series of legislative measures were introduced, mainly targeted at banning access to alcohol which was perceived as the cause of violence: Sporting Events Act 1985, Public Order Act 1986, and Safety of Sports Grounds Act 1987. Influential to the Government's football related legislation was the Popplewell Inquiry which originally set out to investigate the state of safety regulations at football grounds, but at the behest of the Prime Minister:

> ... finished up reading like a contribution to the debate, which was then current in England, on the Police and Criminal Evidence Bill and the extension of police powers of search (I. Taylor, 1991, p.13).

One of its main recommendations was a compulsory membership scheme aimed at combating football violence. This proposal formed Part 1 of the Football Spectators Act 1989, introduced by Colin Moynihan, then Minister for Sport, in January 1989. The second part of the Act concentrated on preventing those previously convicted of 'football related offences' from travelling overseas on days of designated matches. The ID card scheme (as it became known) proposed that anyone entering a football ground when not a member rendered themselves likely to arrest and imprisonment. Again, those previously convicted of football related offences or found to be misbehaving would be disqualified from membership rights.

As Moynihan midwifed the bill through Parliament, opposition from 'official' sources ensured a rocky passage of the most vehement form of legislation designed to sever the links between football and violence. Alan Eastwood, Chairman of the Police Federation, believed the scheme would create more problems than it was trying to solve, while John Stalker, who had taken up a consultancy role on policing football, argued that it would merely displace the violence further. Both the FA and the Football League opposed the introduction of the new technology; Jack Dunnett, then League

President, suggested that the expenditure estimated at £72m to install the machinery did not merit the size of the problem. Instead, football authorities called for a more stringent use of domestic restriction orders in line with the proposals in Part 2 of the Bill. This rebuttal to the Government's proposals led Colin Moynihan to accuse the football authorities of 'Luddite tendencies' in the face of essential modernization. Yet backbench Tories also broke ranks over the ID cards as they recognized the wider electoral implications, fearing the legislation would irritate thousands of working class Tory voters. The football press also vented their fears as to what this "botch of plasticated zeal" (*The Guardian*, 18.1.89) would do to the game. David Lacey, one of the most acerbic commentators on football politics, had the following to say about the Government's "cosmetic exercise" with its "abundance of clanking machinery":

Mrs Thatcher is on the terraces waving the rattle of law and order and demanding a penalty shoot-out. After next season she may have the terraces largely to herself (*The Guardian*, 18.1.89).

Ironically, the Prime Minister was a lone figure on the terraces in the aftermath of Hillsborough in April 1989, as she walked amongst the gnarled and twisted wreckage of the Leppings Lane perimeter fences. The most thorough investigation into the state of British football was set in motion, headed by Lord Justice Taylor. Taylor's interim report apportioned the bulk of the blame on the inadequacy of the police operation. At the beginning of the 89/90 season, mid-way through Lord Justice Taylor's inquiry, Lacey wrote a series of articles entitled 'Soccer Into The Nineties'. Summing up his examination of ID cards and the supporters Lacey concluded:

The spectators - crammed in the Fifties, cajoled in the Sixties, condemned in the Seventies and killed in the Eighties - should be cosseted, not coerced, in the Nineties (*The Guardian*, 10.8.89).

Sympathetic insight into the plight of football fans subsequently formed the majority of Taylor's' final recommendations which showed "grave doubts" about the feasibility of ID cards and "serious misgivings" about its impact on safety. Taylor's opposition to the scheme was premised upon issues of safety and crowd control which he considered relevant to the inquiry given his remit. Although briefly mentioned, arguments related to the loss of residual supporters or the unfairness of implementing such a scheme were not used as major criticisms of the Government's proposals. In effect, what Taylor did, was draw upon 'official discourses' which criticized the scheme on a technical basis, separating this line of argument from the 'popular discourses' of discontent which were overtly political in nature, drawing on criticism raised by the mass of supporters. It is to the influence this groundswell of opinion exerted and the manner in which the FSA and fanzines opposed the ID card scheme that we now turn.

As Lawrence Grossberg (1992) has argued in relation to what he termed 'The affective sensibility of fandom', the power of the popular is an essential ingredient for democratic political struggle to be effectively organized. Fandom, has an enabling or empowering potential. There is no finer example of football fan's political power than the struggle over ID cards. Central government, motivated by the idea of an economically competitive and passive spectator sport, completely misunderstood the productive role fans play in turning a commercial narrative (professional football) into a popular culture. Football fans are textually productive, unlike a theatre audience which shows bourgeois deference between audience and text, fans have a relationship with the game that is active and productive, giving a sense of possession. Rogan Taylor has constantly asserted that fans are integral to the football spectacle. It is fans who make the event.

The 1986/87 season saw the launch of Luton Town's membership scheme which aimed to ban all away support, but only ended up ostracising the club from the rest of the Football League. The clubs Chairman, David Evans, then a prospective Conservative Parliamentary candidate, had acted on the Government's thoughts of introducing membership schemes, after the events of 1985. Not only was the scheme a trial attempt to implement Tory ideas on how to tackle the 'hooligan problem' it was an opportunity for fans to voice their opinion against 'self-appointed moralisers' who had increasing influence on the game. Steve Beauchampe, in October 1986 lambasted the idea of membership schemes, providing an early indication of the opposition that would befall the Government when they introduced their Football Spectators Bill in 1989. He argued:

Luton Town are taking a sledgehammer to crack a nut, and quite frankly, there is no point in supporting a 'solution' if it is obviously stupid ... As the first club to make supporting their team a condition of entry, Luton's gross infringement of personal liberty and free speech so enthusiastically supported by the police has nothing whatsoever to do with the ideals and principles of football spectatorship. And now, having banned everyone else, the mad Hatters are banned themselves, hoisted on their own petard, they don't like it. Imagine the outrage if it was proposed to place a curfew on men going out at night in an attempt to stop rape. David Evans might have something to say about that (*Off The Ball*, October/November 1986).

Ironically, the Luton scheme became a shambles as reports of visiting fans gaining entry into the ground became known. Some estimate that as many as 1000 Chelsea supporters, some wearing club colours singing and chanting as normal, gained entry to Kenilworth Road under false pretences. Moreover, in what was then Luton's most successful season near the top of Division One, average League gates fell by almost 1000. In an updated report 'Luton - One Year On', Beauchampe translated the feelings among Luton fans themselves:

Most Luton fans would like to see some easing of the restrictions, many want them scrapped. The improved facilities, the roofing of the old away end, and the removal of most of the fences and police are all welcome, but don't compensate for the unreal atmosphere engendered by the presence of a few suppressed away fans, the artificial pitch, and the sight of a row of bloody holiday chalets down one side of the ground (*Off The Ball*, June/July 1987).

Beauchampe, and indeed many Luton fans, were hopeful that restrictions would be eased the following season. However, more generally, fears that a national ID card scheme would be implemented were growing, and were eventually realized when the Tory government were re-elected in 1987 and Colin Moynihan was proclaimed Minister for Sport in 1988.

A certain amount of fatalism grasped many commentators as they saw the implementation of ID cards as inevitable - the best that could be hoped for was a watering-down of the proposed legislation, unveiled in January 1989. Such pessimism took its roots from a decade of Thatcherism, and a government that had achieved a host of crushing defeats on any social movements in opposition to its politics.

Violent disturbances at the 1988 European Championships involving English fans in Germany saw a high profile Colin Moynihan MP determined to carry through legislation to curb 'hooliganism', which would be a prerequisite for English clubs to return into European club competition. A Working Party on Football: National Membership Schemes was set-up, its final report forming the basis of future legislation without recourse to a White Paper. With football high on the agenda and fanzines multiplying rapidly, there emerged a rare opportunity for cultural consumers to report and document in detail the supposed democratic process of the British Parliamentary system. Moreover, the FSA had tapped its resources and contacts in the media to increase the profile of the 'fan lobby'. The FSA conducted a survey on ID cards amongst their members in the 1987/88 season and found that for most clubs the scheme was impractical, irrelevant, and potentially dangerous. In September 1988 Rogan Taylor and Craig Brewin proposed an alternative viewpoint as to what the word 'membership' should mean when they wrote:

> If compulsory ID cards become law, we will exert every pressure to achieve a genuine 'membership' that gives supporters rights as well as responsibilities (*WSC*, No. 19).

John Duncan of *WSC* also highlighted the sweeping and indiscriminate nature of ID cards when he argued:

> The central tenet of the scheme is that it has to be universal to be effective. That is the justification for punishing even those clubs and supporters who have a tiny arrest rate per season. This blind devotion to an unselective principle is the most illogical thing about the scheme (*WSC*, No. 23).

Duncan provided extensive coverage of the legislation process leading up to the Football Spectators Act 1989. In March 1989, he investigated the viewpoints of various MPs who had spoken out on the scheme. This not only highlighted who opposed the scheme, but who was in favour and readers were urged to write to their MP.

All social movements/pressure groups have their 'freeloaders'. Football fans traditionally compliant due to the extensive coercive practices of the police, have not been the most vociferous campaigning group or politically rebellious. But the ID card scheme produced an unprecedented feeling of resentment and frustration that those in parliamentary power were deciding the future of the national game without consultation with its consumers, the fans. Beside the letters to MPs and articles in fanzines, numerous public meetings were held, and on the terraces numerous banners, T-shirts, and badges began to appear with the clear message 'NO TO ID CARDS'. One notable example of opposition came from Guy Lovelady of the fanzine *Rodney Rodney* and devout Manchester City fan who cleverly twisted the Maine Road inflatables craze with the banner 'ID CARDS? BANANAS!'. *Rodney Rodney* also had Brian McClair of Manchester United, one of the more politically active professional footballers, adorn the front cover of Issue 4 wearing an FSA T-shirt proudly stating 'Fans Say NO to ID Cards'.

More radical and vehement protestations came from a fanzine called *LOUD* which used the inflammatory headline 'Moynihan You Are Scum' to express their feelings in no uncertain terms. The fanzine printed the home address of Colin Moynihan and there followed reports that the Minister had received death threats and excrement through the post. The Tory press came out in sympathy for the Minister for Sport, Ian Wooldridge of the *Daily Mail* (27.6.89) revealing the 'venomous campaign' under the headline 'Colin Moynihan's Ordeal By Terror'.

However, not even this negative coverage of fan opposition could deflect the spirit and humour with which the FSA and fanzines fought the campaign against the scheme. It was humour that proved to be a key ingredient in the social politics of football fandom. To a degree fanzines were preaching to the converted. Because the fans had 'heard it all before' new creative ways of expressing opposition to the Government were vital. Moynihan, whose diminutive figure served him well as a cox in an Olympic Rowing team before indulging himself in politics, became the centre of ridicule. He was no longer the Minister for Sport but the 'Miniature for Sport'. After observing debates on football in the House of Commons, John Duncan suggested that MPs showed a touch more subtlety when trying to undermine the opposition. He writes:

The masterful Dennis Howell would never stoop to calling Mr Moynihan 'shortie' of course. He preferred to remark that "if the Minister has ever been to a football match, he can never have seen anything". In the good old days, of course, Mr Moynihan would have been freely passed from shoulder to shoulder on every terrace in the country. Nowadays he probably satisfies himself with a large cushion in the directors box (*WSC*, No. 19).

Other erudite passages appeared on the letters page of *WSC*, like the following from Nigel Glenn of Nottingham:

Colin Moynihan's name, rearranged and with a few letters added, spells out A Horrible little Weasel Of A Man. Incredible eh? (*WSC*, No. 27).

And this surreal vagary from Adrian Briggs, of Oxford:

Has anyone noticed that Thatch's instructions to Noddy are concealed within 'Colin Moynihan, The Small But Perfectly formed Minister Of Sport', namely 'Reform It Child Prince, Minister Shitlump, nasty Enemy of Football!' Or is the pressure beginning to get to me? (*WSC*, No. 27).

The fanzine *A Love Supreme* (Sunderland) asked the question 'Colin Moynihan - What's his Game?' which was comically answered with a photograph of the Minister and a bubble caption which read "I'm from Mars". The disbelief that ID cards could be introduced to control one of the nation's major pastimes motivated the fanzine *Blow Football* (Subbuteo/general) to suggest that Moynihan (nicknamed 'Mr Half-Pint') would introduce a "Lager Drinkers bill". In a make-believe article, under the heading 'Beer On The Cards' the article quoted "Mr Colin Half-Pint, the Minister for Alcohol" as saying:

Lager drinking has become tarnished by the violence caused by a number of its participants. We want to go back to the good old days when lager drinking was a family activity, and Britain had the best empire the world has ever seen (*Blow Football*, No. 2).

By juxtaposing the cultural spheres of football and drinking the article throws back into the face of Tory Government its own persistence of applying a rigorous economic and moral ideology into myriad spheres of civil society (see Hall, 1988).

The wide and deeply felt opposition to ID cards, which was sustained and resolute, gained a sympathetic hearing in Lord Justice Taylor's Final Report. The influence of the unwavering stance of the FSA and fanzines on Taylor's opinion on membership schemes should not be understated. The backing down of the Prime Minister on the issue of membership schemes was due in no small measure to the campaigning by 'ordinary' football fans, although tragically, the prime catalyst for the Governments U-turn were the deaths at Hillsborough.

Blow Football celebrated the demise of the 'Miniature for Sport' with the headline 'Moynihan's gone!' (Issue 5) and sarcastically commented "God help the Department of Energy". Yet, Part 1 of the Football Spectators Act 1989, has only been shelved. Only six months after Taylor's final report, Annie Bassett, the Chief Executive of Birmingham City, announced that the club were introducing their own computerized card scheme. In disbelief the local FSA submitted a request for the safety certificate at St Andrews to be withdrawn, reiterating Taylor's opposition to such an idea. However, the submission was rejected and the scheme went ahead as planned. Steve Moss voiced his disbelief arguing:

> Ms Bassett, no doubt, was one of those tut-tutting when the little boy pointed out that The Emperor's New Clothes didn't exist. Or maybe Birmingham City are a front organisation for The Flat Earth Society. Whatever, you have been warned - the ID card argument is not dead yet, and the legislation is still on the statute book (*Blow Football*, No. 5).

This is a sobering thought for those fans who thought they had seen the last of the ID card scheme. Lord Justice Taylor's Final Report did force the Government's hand on the implementation of the scheme, but the idea is certain to resurface during a fourth term of Tory government. Taylor's own recommendations of all-seater stadia have further divided opinion amongst supporters on the way ahead for the professional game. Indeed, all seater stadia, now a panacea for all football's ills in the eyes of the Government and football administrators, has given birth to a host of independent supporters' organisations attempting to have their say in the way clubs modernize. It is to the political relationship between fans and the clubs they support we now turn, both pre- and post-Hillsborough.

"You're not standing anymore!"

Chants like 'sack the board' have become common cries from football terraces in the 80s and 90s. A single chant or sign of disapproval from a mass of football fans conveys the message of discontent far more immediately than any fanzine article could hope to achieve. Fanzines have, however, supported, sustained and often channelled this ground swell of opinion and anger. Like all forms of hatred - which is what the relationship between fans and those who control English football frequently amounts to - football fan vitriol is born of fear. Fear that things 'ain't what they used to be', fear that historical and community ties could be smashed in an instant, fear that the club they support might not exist in a year's/month's/week's time and that they are being priced out of a game that was once a readily affordable form of entertainment.

The impact of the Taylor Report has come at a time of deep economic recession. Yet football has been experiencing its own recession since the 70s, which was compounded after Heysel. Ambitious chairmen have always been more likely to spend their millions on players that cut bank deficits or rebuild sections of the ground. The irony is that fans are often complicit with the 'win at all costs' mentality eschewed by the chairman at the expense of better facilities. But since the mid 80s football's finances have threatened the Saturday afternoon rituals of the fans like never before. Clubs, faced with one financial crisis after another, became assets from which to make a fast buck, to float on the financial markets and for bank managers to call in the receiver.

These economic pressures were most evident in London where football clubs were sucked into the 80s development boom. An idea that found favour among some of the capital's football administrators and senior management, most notably Ron Noades of Crystal Palace, were mergers. Asset stripping had become a boom industry under the Tory Government and now it was football's turn. In 1987 two such mergers were proposed: Crystal Palace and Wimbledon (who would vacate Plough Lane) and Fulham and QPR (who would be renamed Fulham Park Rangers). These radical propositions were met by an equally radical opposition from supporters. A cross-club supporters' organization was quickly formed, called the Football in London Action Group (FLAG), guided by the FSA. Meetings and demonstrations were organized, in what came to be the FSA's first show of strength in its ability to mobilize supporters from different clubs, over an issue which had wider ramifications for the game as a whole. Although these mergers were defeated, financial problems still befell a number of clubs involved, most notably Fulham.

In August 1988 Cabra Estates the landlords of Fulham FC's ground Craven Cottage unveiled plans to demolish three quarters of the ground for redevelopment, including among other things, a couple of thousand executive flats. The Stevenage Road stand and the Craven Cottage, two listed Edwardian buildings designed by Archie Leitch, would remain as part of a neoclassical development designed by Quinlan Terry. The proposals were soon vilified by the fans. The fanzine *There's Only One F In Fulham* stated in its editorial:

> Of course, to you and me these plans are complete flights of fancy and totally outside the guidelines laid down by the Council in their planning brief. However, one never knows and it is down to every single Fulham supporter to ensure that these ridiculous notions are booted, once and for all, into touch (*There's Only One F In Fulham*, Issue 3).

Graffiti soon emerged around the ground stating "END OF FULHAM, END OF FOOTBALL" and the fans' predicament gained sympathy. As hinted earlier in the above editorial the local authority, Fulham and Hammersmith Council, were also wary of the development. The council's legal advisors sought a compulsory purchase order, allowing the council to rent the ground back to the club as landlords. However, in 1991 speculations as to the future of Craven Cottage were laid to rest when Jimmy Hill, Fulham's Chairman, sold the lease on the ground for £13m to Cabra Estates. Hill was adamant that he could not refuse the offer, believing a new purpose built stadium on another site was necessary to comply with the recommendations of the Taylor report. But the high cost of land in West London has made the relocation of the club within the London borough an impossibility. Fifteen hundred fans, devastated by the news, held a peaceful protest on the pitch during the half-time interval of a Third Division game with Notts County, chanting "We'll never leave the Cottage!". After fears that they would have to vacate the ground Fulham continued to play out the 92/93 season at the Cottage.

Craven Cottage according to Simon Inglis is architecturally an important part of British social history. More specifically in relation to the clubs' fans it signifies an emotional bond with a regular place of pilgrimage. John Bale (1991) has typified this tie between supporters and football stadiums as a form of 'topophilia', which in the football context, is "the situations in which football 'couples sentiment with place' ". In the above case of Fulham 'topophilia' generated a sense of loss, but more recently in the case of Charlton Athletic, this form of 'topophilic loss' has been overturned to signify a sense of homecoming.

In 1985 the club distributed leaflets to its supporters stating that there would only be one more game at The Valley, the home of Charlton Athletic. Fans were notified that the club was due to share the facilities of Crystal Palace and sensing they had some form of obligation to the fans, gave brief directions on how to get to Selhurst Park. The reasons for the move were ambiguous but centred around post-Bradford fire and safety regulations and the desire of a former chairman, Michael Gliksten, to develop his share of the property at The Valley. Fans were not only outraged at the lack of consultation but considerably aggrieved that they had to leave a place that "had run like a thread through their lives" (quoted in Bale, 1991, p.133). So began the long, political battle to return to The Valley by Charlton supporters. The fanzine *Voice Of The Valley* edited by Rick Everitt provided a constant 'thorn in the side' of those who opposed the idea of ever recovering the old ground as it gradually fell into disrepair. Crystal Palace were saving £90,000 a year out of the ground share while Charlton were losing an estimated £500,000 a year because of the drop in attendances. In many respects the deficit was due to the distance fans had to travel across London for home games, and further, to the lack of affective ties between the fans and the club's new surroundings. Because of the losses the club incurred, plus the mounting pressure exerted by the fans, in 1989 Charlton's board decided to submit a proposal to return to The Valley to Greenwich Council. Ironically, two days after the publication of the Taylor Report in January 1990, Charlton's plans to move to an all-seater stadium at The Valley were opposed by the local authority. The local planning authority objected to the plans because of the nuisance that fans posed to local residents. This rejection motivated supporters into explicit political action with the formation of the Valley Party. The Party contested sixty seats, receiving extensive media coverage on local TV and radio. A massive poster campaign was launched from a billboard advertisement proclaiming "REMEMBER WHEN YOU WERE PROUD TO COME FROM CHARLTON?" accompanied by a photograph from Charlton's last FA Cup victory, to smaller posters which suggested "Lets send the Council to Croydon and see how they like it". Funding for the campaign came from the Supporters' Club (£4000), *Voice Of The Valley* (£500), and independent donations (£2000). An 0898 phone-in was set up to give up to date information on the latest news 'from the front' as polling day loomed, in May 1990. In another advertisement the Valley Party gave the following message to their supporters:

> This campaign has already united the football club, the supporters and the community as never before. But now we must prove it to the politicians on the streets of Greenwich .... We've done our bit. Now it's up to you. If you care, you'll be there.

The unprecedented manoeuvre of entering into the local political arena eventually paid off as Greenwich Council agreed to process the club's application. Construction of a 17,000 all-seater stadium, estimated at a cost of £9m, was expected to be completed during the 1992-93 season. Finally, the improved links and consultation between the club and the fans has led to the establishment of a fan/director to oversee the club's return to The Valley in December 1992.

The modernization of the game has brought into question the depth of emotion and sense of place many fans have for their club. Ideas of building multi-purpose, all-seater stadiums on green field sites away from the historical location of grounds within inner cities has divided opinion between those in positions of power and the fans. When the chairman of Hearts, Wallace Mercer, launched a £6.1m take-over bid for fellow Edinburgh club Hibernian, he miscalculated the depth of feeling among fans from both sides. The requirements of the Taylor report and the shifting structure of European football had motivated Mercer to attempt the merger. After revealing his plans the Hearts chairman stated:

Hearts is capable of financing the construction of a new stadium but it believes in uniting the clubs to provide a stronger financial basis for the future ... The challenge is there. Some of us have to pick up the gauntlet and run with it (*The Independent*, 5.6.90).

However, this 'gauntlet' was picked up by the Hibs fans who rose to Mercer's challenge by creating the campaign 'Hands Off Hibs'. The Hibs fanzine *The Proclaimer* took upon itself the role of disseminating as much information about the campaign as possible. In September 1990 the fanzine explained how it had foretold the likely outcome of the club's financial problems:

For over a year, *The Proclaimer* stood almost alone in warning how vulnerable Hibernian was to a take-over bid. Only the source of the bid came as a surprise. While Saddam Hussain was mobilising his troops to annexe Kuwait Wallace Mercer was checking out Hibernians plc share register (*The Proclaimer*, Issue 11).

The traditional and bitter rivalry between the two Edinburgh clubs was heightened as both sets of supporters wanted to maintain their identity. Protest was fierce throughout June and July 1990, a petition was raised and presented to the Prime Minister with the backing of numerous Scottish MPs. The intense lobbying finally paid off as the merger was scrapped before the start of the 90/91 season. The first encounter between the two clubs at Easter Road, home of Hibs, saw fans celebrating their independence by twice invading the pitch during the match. Further celebration came with the release of a 4-track 12" EP 'Victory' which included songs by the supporters club and the Scottish duo The Proclaimers.

Although the 'Hands Off Hibs' campaign was successful, *The Proclaimer* continued to push for further fan representation. The club and the supporters had joined forces to defeat the merger but the club's future was still in financial crisis. Tensions remained between the board and the fans as *The Proclaimer* aimed to correct the imbalance of power between what it termed "two irreconcilable partners". The fanzine argued:

In defeating Mercer's bid lets not forget that first and foremost the most important role was played by the fans themselves - were it not for their outcry, people like Tom Farmer [who stepped in to save the club] would not have come forward, business would not have concerned themselves with being seen to be on the right side of the argument and Mercer would have been able to go ahead. The fans acted as the trigger for the chain of events that saved Hibs (*The Proclaimer*, Vol. 2, Issue 1).

The fanzine subsequently set out a six point plan for "The Way Forward" the main argument being that "there is absolutely no reason to sell our principal asset - Easter Road stadium." The fanzine proposed building a new ground on the same site, with the use of adjacent derelict land owned by the local council. More than anything the Hibs/Hearts saga, and the defiant stance to maintain Easter Road as a sporting venue, represents an exceptional capacity for football fans to play a proactive role in the future of their own club and the game as a whole.

The move towards creating a fan/club dialogue through representation or consultation has been a major objective of the FSA. The 1991/92 season provided another set of conflicts that prompted unprecedented political activity by football fans. The FA's *Blueprint For The Future Of Football* and the unveiling of ground developments by numerous clubs augured a series of counter-proposals and defensive measures by fans both nationally and locally.

Despite the work and progressive initiatives the FSA and the independent supporters' organizations had achieved during the late 80s and early 90s, the clubs and the FA conceived and produced their proposals from within their ivory tower. This ignorant and damning contempt of supporters' opinions, post-Hillsborough, forced the FSA into action and created a new series of independent club organizations. In the introduction to an alternative document on the future of football, *The Supporters Blueprint*, the FSA suggested:

... if the events of 1991 demonstrate anything, it is that there can be no such thing as a hard and fast Blueprint for the Future of Football. There are too many competing and conflicting interests, too many compromises to be made, and too many people unwilling to do as they are told by *Bluprint* authors. However, what is clear is that regardless of the suggestions being put forward, the supporters voice should be heard.

A major draft proposal was a restructuring of the Football League, written by John Tummon, which aimed at creating, among other objectives, "equal chances for all" under the philosophy that "The new Football League must re-assert the centrality of sporting values" (Tummon 1991). Such 'Corinthian' values are riddled with contradictions - not least because of the media saturated, sponsorship led world of sport - but it does stand in stark contrast to the overtly elitist and insular philosophy of the FA Premier League which is purely founded on greed. Indeed, the major claim that the Premier League will benefit the national side has so far been hopelessly unfounded as fixtures are as crammed as ever and Graham Taylor's side is continually dogged by injury.

The complexities of Tummon's proposal are too detailed to be outlined here, but the emphasis was on a radical, dynamic and highly mobile structure which would ensure a rapid flow of teams between the League structure. But do such radical proposals stand much chance of success? Or will they remain whims of fancy? Do such proposals represent the opinion of the majority of supporters? Herein lies a major problem for the FSA. Although the FSA has been instrumental in motivating campaigns, creating a more proactive approach by fans as to the way the game is controlled, it will always face the problem of representation. Ideas about creating a football 'ombudsfan' to liaise with the necessary agencies is fraught with complications, most of which centre around democracy.

The rise of independent supporter's organizations - Off The Shelf (Spurs), Arsenal Independent Supporters Association against the bond scheme, West Ham United fans against a bond scheme, to name but a few - have highlighted the restrictive nature of some aspects in the FSA organization. Individual club issues often over-ride the broader view, a fans' loyalty to and most of all, knowledge of the club often provide more realistic options for forcing the club's hand than grander schemes put forward by the non-partisan, non-parochial FSA.

Manchester United's Supporters Association (USA) previously known as HOSTAGE is a case in point. USA was established to contend the clubs financial grounds for unprecedented increases in the price of tickets. Although their inaugural meeting at Old Trafford Cricket ground in February 1992 included representatives of other independent supporter's associations and the FSA who were categorically opposed to all-seater stadiums, USA's prime target was pricing policy. USA's leaders considered the ideas of the FSA to be unrealistic, and likened them to a bunch of "dreamers". They believe the FSA have got their politics wrong and have misjudged the all-seater debate, i.e. despite being successful in overturning the Government's ID card scheme, the all-seater policy is a "different kettle of fish". Protests like releasing hundreds of red balloons (circa West Ham fans) or sitting on the terraces and standing on the seats were considered inappropriate to Manchester United. Red cards, as a means of protest, were used at the game with Coventry at Highfield Road, but at the request of the FSA. Indeed, USA conceded to United's board that all-seater stadiums were inevitable, and although it meant the last of the Stretford End, the supporter's association were happy that the club would have been willing to keep some of the 'paddocks' open for standing if their hands had not been tied by the Taylor Report. USA's prime objective was to hit the club financially, a tall order considering United made the largest profit for any League club in 1991/92 (£5.4m). By presenting the board with an alternative set of figures, suggesting that the increase in prices was unfair, USA then hatched a plan to devalue United's share price by persuading a major shareholder to 'dump' their shares on the market. However, this plan proved equally unrealistic, but did signify another way in which fans could exert pressure on the club they support. The financial buoyancy of United and their enormous following across the country (if not the world), has made USA's task all the more daunting. The fanzines *Red Issue* and *United We Stand* were involved in the campaign, acting as the mouthpiece of the fan lobby, and distributing membership forms to join USA in their March issues. They also organized a petition to be presented to the club. Yet the two fanzines' most successful initiative to undermine the club has been the organization of coaches for away matches which undercut the clubs 'official' away excursions which were considered to be overpriced and too inflexible. These smaller, but significant interventions show the immediate future of football fan politics. They are premised on a sense of justice, something which many fans would argue has been conspicuous by its absence within the game of football.

To return to the all-seater debate, Ian Taylor (1991) has argued that the defence of terrace culture by fanzines - standing in the pouring rain, eating rancid meat pies and joining in the crude banter of fellow supporters - depicts a 'fantastic' representation of the fan's actual experience. This is a crucial argument if fan politics are to continue opposing all-seater stadiums. It must be accepted that many fanzines are guilty of wearing 'rose tinted glasses', nostalgia is often a major component in fanzine discourse. Yet chauvinistic and sexist behaviour or chanting is as likely to come from the seats as the terraces. The point is that terracing can be improved by roofing, wider gangways and reduction of capacity, recommendations that have been pushed for by fanzines but have fallen on deaf ears. As North Bank Norman of *Fortunes Always Hiding* (West Ham) has suggested about the situation at Upton park:

> West Ham doesn't need more seats and certainly not at the expense of fewer fans. Upton Park is a good ground that needs a little care and attention, not the heart ripping from it ... We don't have fences and trouble inside is rare. Anyone who thinks seats stop hooliganism should watch a video of the Luton v Millwall game that so terrified our Prime Minister. The hail of square blue objects which rained down on the police were seats (*Fortunes Always Hiding*, Issue 5).

We have come full circle! The Taylor Report ignores the fact that capacities in nearly all League grounds have been drastically reduced over the last twenty years, often by 50%. The football establishment, central and local government have accepted Taylor's recommendations without debate. The views of the supporters have not been sought, whereas their interest on these issues should be paramount. The new FA Premier League and the Football League could lead on this by asking their clubs to establish a dialogue with their supporters.

7   We hate Jimmy Hill: The relationship between football, fanzines and television

When we were launched it was the end of modern civilisation, Christendom and life as we know it (Dave Hill, executive producer, Sky Eurosport [*The Independent on Sunday*, 2.9.90]).

One of the major tenets fanzine editors and writers proclaim to be an influential and motivating factor in producing a fanzine is their antagonism towards the coverage of football on television. The banal self-parodying of Messrs. *Saint and Greavsie* throughout the late 80s and early 90s has provided more than enough material to highlight the shortcomings of televised football to show that it is not always 'a funny old game'. Yet the above mentioned programme has generated its own form of popularity drawing upon the satirical attention it receives from fanzines and the likes of the mimicking puppets on *Spitting Image* . The format of football on television is, however, a highly contentious and seriously debated issue with competing and contradictory discourses. The main focus of the debate is the 'marketability' of the game as a 'product' to be sold to a globalized media whose audience is increasingly 'media literate' aware of the widening scope of 'home entertainment' as alternatives to terrestrial television.

   From the early sixties television has been the prime medium for developing the enthusiasm of a young audience (invariably male) to the pleasure and pain of professional football. As Garry Whannel (1983, p.58) succinctly put it about sport in general: "Nowadays, for most people most of the time, sports means televised sport". Football in the UK can now expect to have aggregate viewing figures in excess of 400 million per year.

Italia '90 marked a watershed for football as televised spectacle. Previous World Cups, particularly the tournament held in England in 1966, had illustrated that televised football could reach a broader audience beyond the committed fan. Exploiting the potentially massive world-wide audience for *Italia '90* and all the benefits which sponsors and advertisers could accrue, FIFA negotiated £33.6m. in TV rights for 60 hours of football. The host nation Italy's opening game against the USA had 30 million Italians glued to their sets, representing 80% of the country's viewing audience. However it was England's relative success in the 1990 World Cup that came to signify the turning point in the game's media image. The World Cup semi-final between England and West Germany drew an armchair audience of 25 million (the largest audience for a single event in the history of British TV). The game's allure was boosted considerably, increasing the bargaining power of the football authorities after televised football in England had reached its nadir after the tragedy at Heysel. Football was 'off the box' for the majority of the 85-86 season, dealing a considerable blow to the clubs who were in need of shirt sponsorship and perimeter advertising.

Narratives of the bargaining wrangles between football and television, and within the media itself have been documented elsewhere (Geraghty, Simpson and Whannel 1986; Wagg and Goldberg 1991). Suffice to say that ITV's exclusive deal with the Football League of £44m. over four years in 1988, which broke the cartel between themselves and the BBC which had previously kept the price of football down, has since had a profound effect on the coverage of English football, in both cost and presentation. However what has not been adequately documented is the relationship between football TV programmes, their perceived audience and the rise of a 'culture of defence' among fans.

These complex relations are exemplified in the recent discourses on football and television surrounding the new FA Premier League. As far back as the late sixties there were musings of a 'Super-League within a League' due to the growing gulf between 'bigger' and 'smaller' clubs. The early work of Ian Taylor (1970) had recognized such a fact when he was theorizing about the loss of 'participatory democracy' by fans in the face of "soccer as a passive form of commercial exchange and 'entertainment'" as envisaged by directors, sponsors and the mass media. The same discourses appear today but the stakes are much higher as the game is engulfed in global, media saturated processes of the cultural industries.

On 18 May 1992, the newly formed Premier League accepted a joint television package put forward by the BBC and the satellite company BSkyB worth £304m over five years. The main negotiator in the deal on *behalf* of football was Rick Parry an accountant brought in on a short term contract as chief executive of the Premier League. On the confirmation of the deal Parry announced: "It will be the first time football has had a voice in the way the sport is covered on television" (*The Guardian* 19.5.92).

The crux of this argument lies behind the revenue the Premier League is likely to reap from a 'pay-to-view' channel dedicated to football, from which they will share 50% of BSkyB receipts. Live games will be encapsulated in a five hour long programme, with promises of analysis of previous games, styles of play and tactics. This format, Parry believes, will outstrip the joke ridden *Saint and Greavsie* and the "slab coverage" offered by *The Match* (*The Guardian*, 28.5.92).

The snub that ITV received from the Premier League has several interesting narratives, from both within and without the television industry. Of particular interest are comments in relation to the perceived 'interest' of armchair football fans. We shall begin with the people directly involved in the deal for the Premier League. At the loss of the deal Greg Dyke chairman of the ITV Association and head of ITV Sport came out in a show of sympathy for the TV fan. He proclaimed:

> I feel more strongly about the loss to viewers than about the commercial issue. I feel strongly for the people like my dad who was a devoted football fan and who would never have bought a dish and who wouldn't be able to see the game anymore (*The Guardian* 25.5.92).

However Dyke had shown no signs of sentimentality or Luddite views towards the evolving world of communications when he had secured ITV's deal in 1988. Through Dyke's commercial vigour ITV had set out with their programme, *The Match* , to 'revolutionize' football coverage, by providing a thrilling spectacle to stem the tide of a perceived apathy among the public about hum-drum soccer watching. New camera angles were sought and developed over the four year life span of *The Match* , players and managers were grabbed for touchline interviews as they emerged from the tunnel or were retreating from a dismal display. Part of the rationale behind the new style presentation were the needs of advertising who foresaw ITV's audience as too old, too female and too working class. The introduction of *The Match* as a glossier form of entertainment would hopefully attract an audience higher up the socioeconomic scale, boosting viewing figures and ultimately attract the custom of advertisers. The new style of coverage appeared to work as viewing figures for live football increased. When Arsenal clinched the title against Liverpool at Anfield in 1989, the audience of 10.3m was greater than BBC's audience for the FA Cup Final of that year. The then editor of *The Match* Jeff Farmer argued:

> We have been criticised for concentrating on the major clubs, but the audiences are an absolute justification that these are the matches the public wants. Sunday afternoon and *The Match* are becoming as much part of Sunday as a pint down the local and Sunday lunch (*The Independent*, January 1990).

ITV Sport knew they were on to a successful formula, with average audiences of 7m and peaks of more than 10m. ITV went into negotiations for the Premier League on the understanding that their bid of £265m and their track record in covering live football would secure the contract. The bewilderment of losing out on the Premier League coverage to a late bid by the BBC/BSkyB partnership was followed by the allegation that the Premier League's chief executive had committed a breach of confidence by informing ITV's competitors of their bid. ITV attempted to gain an injunction on the final decision on the contract to give themselves time to resubmit a further bid. However, this legal attempt to fight back was in vain. ITV then made further allegations of impropriety in a letter to the director-general at the Office of Fair Trading, Sir Gordon Borrie, suggesting that Rupert Murdoch's promise of the full support of his newspapers had influenced the voting by the Premier League Committee. Dyke was reported as saying:

> We believe this finally proves that the concentration of cross-media interests at News International has become anti-competitive and is distorting the market (*The Times*, 23.5.92).

102

Rick Parry later refuted the claims that Murdoch had guaranteed favourable editorial coverage, suggesting the main criterion for rejecting ITV's bid was the TV company's rejection of a Premier League 'pay channel' to be broadcast in conjunction with ITV.

A crucial aspect of the conflict between ITV and the satellite company stems from the Broadcasting Act 1990. For many years ITV had enjoyed a monopoly on TV advertisements, enabling them to inflate the price of commercials much to the dismay of advertisers themselves. The 1990 Act was a continuation of Thatcherite ideology to increase competition within as many industrial spheres as possible. The Act recognized the potential of the emerging technology of satellite communications to introduce competition within the TV industry, lessening the burden on advertisers, eventually leading to an improved model of a market economy. The market would ensure the most efficient companies would win broadcasting rights through the auctioning of franchises. The Act also ensured that the Government would receive revenue by imposing a tax for granting the right to broadcast. ITV clearly resented the fact that their companies face an overall bill in excess of £300m for their licence to broadcast and lost the Premier League deal to a satellite company that is barely regulated, has no programme quotas, does not have to pay the Government anything and was in partnership with a government sponsored agency: the BBC. This last fact proved to be the major criticism over the Premier League debacle as perceived by ITV Sports producers.

Since the inter-war years BBC (radio and TV) had covered sport under the remit of being the 'nation's voice' assimilating people to the belief in a single nation culture. BBC sports coverage became an icon of its corporate prestige. A government agreement that stated that neither BBC nor ITV could obtain exclusive coverage of certain listed events (FA Cup Final, Wimbledon, the Boat Race, the Derby, the Grand National and test cricket) worked to reinforce BBC's dominance because ITV found it hard to compete for audiences when both sides covered an event due to breaks for adverts. The liberal (social democratic) tenet that underlies much of BBC's policies was thrown back in the Corporation's face after the Premier League deal. Under the heading "A disastrous own goal for the BBC" (*The Observer*, 24/5/92), controller of Arts at LWT, Melvyn Bragg, pronounced his disbelief at the "bewildering alliance" struck up between BBC and BSkyB. The apparent short-termism of the BBC deal with satellite was seen to demonstrate a lack of commercial judgment, a decision more applicable to the TV battles of the 70s and not the 90s, giving a considerable boost to the BBC's own demise. Moreover, universality of access had now been denied by the very agency that had prided itself in being a public service broadcaster. For this reason Bragg argued:

The BBC policy makers must have decided - admittedly at a surprisingly late stage - that they wanted above all to damage ITV, not clearly, to serve that large proportion of the British public - of which I declare myself an avid member - for which football is an important part of their lives (*The Observer*, 24.5.92).

This opinion was echoed by 'impresario' Michael Grade, Chief Executive of Channel 4 who added:

The BBC may hope that partnership with the Murdoch empire will soften the edges of the leaders and comment in the News International papers during its argument with government for the renewal of the BBC charter and licence. That is a short-term gain to be measured against long-term suicide (*The Guardian*, 23.5.92).

There was also disquiet among independent TV commentators over the Government's seemingly apathetic attitude over the rights to the Premier League. David Mellor, the newly appointed Secretary of the Department for Heritage, refused to intervene after being prompted by several MP's to hold an inquiry. Mellor, whose popular culture credentials of being a Chelsea fan were heavily lauded before the General Election, bowed out of any discussion on the matter of the BBC's 'betrayal' of public service broadcasting ideals. This was characteristic of government policies, set out in the 1990 Act, to put the market and viewer's choice ahead of regulatory imposition. On this point Grade concluded:

This is a funny concept of choice: allowing BSkyB to take what's available for free and offer it to the same consumers at a monthly cost (*The Guardian*, 23.5.92).

It could be argued that the 'free' viewing of ITV is passed on via consumer goods and services because of the cost of TV advertising. But the point to be made is that there is a contradictory process occurring, whereby a perceived increase in choice is complemented by a greater concentration of ownership in the guise of News International who were given free reign by government to develop their cross-media interests.

A further twist to the Premier League saga was an outcry among certain member clubs and managers of the newly formed league itself. Arsenal, Everton, Leeds United, Liverpool and Manchester United all voiced their opposition to Premier League chief executive, Rick Parry, over the new TV deal. Howard Wilkinson, chairman of the Football Managers Association, opposed the deal on the grounds that Monday night games would disrupt English clubs in European competition. This sentiment was echoed by Jim Greenwood, Everton's chief executive, who was quoted as saying:

> Bearing in mind that there will be no Premier League football on four Saturdays next season, it is conceivable that our leading clubs, if successful, could be faced by a situation where they have only a handful of Saturday games during the course of a ten month period. That would be ridiculous and totally unfair on supporters who quite rightly regard football as a Saturday afternoon pastime (*The Times*, 23.5.92).

Despite such fears the majority of the clubs accepted the deal Parry had negotiated on their behalf. BSkyB have argued they do not want the 'Big Five' on television every week, calculating that fourteen clubs will have one Monday match a season, the eight others two. There are also considerations of allowing managers an input into fixture scheduling. However, clubs would rather not play any games on Monday nights and with the police also commanding a say in the scheduling of matches the power of managers in the decision-making process is further diminished. Which teams appear on live TV and the distribution of money from such matches has always been hotly disputed. Ken Bates, chairman of Chelsea, had previously banned cameras from Stamford Bridge in January 1990, claiming copyright on all the clubs' home games in defiance of the poor distribution of TV revenue between First Division clubs. The revenue expected from the Premier League's 50% share of a 'pay-to-view' channel is another subject likely to cause disruption. The money could either be spread across all clubs or just those involved in live games. Overall, the Premier League clubs can expect to receive a substantial sum of money for TV rights, some estimating receipts to equal the amounts taken at the turnstiles.

Armchair supporters and fanzines

But what of the benefits to the fan? For football fanatics (read male TV addicts) the major benefit of satellite coverage is the amount of sport available on a single channel. Sport can be shown on BSkyB throughout the day unlike terrestrial channels which have to fit in drama, news, quiz shows etc. It is the over-saturation of football on television that has been a persistent fear in the back of the minds of football clubs and fans who attend matches themselves. The fans are needed for televised football to work, if the ground is empty the game ceases to be a spectacle as the event is starved of atmosphere. For this reason fans hold a latent power, however small, in the decision making process of football on television. As viewers, fans have the right to turn off their TV sets or simply not purchase satellite dishes. But this is small comfort for the committed football follower. Watching the game in the pub is one remedy, and is a course of action that has proved popular in Scotland for cup and league games shown on satellite. The obvious advantage to the fan is the beer and the added atmosphere that is absent from the comfort of the home. However, the Premier League deal is clearly targeted at the domestic market - the satellite companies do not want to give something away for nothing! A further consequence of the BSkyB deal could be an actual increase in attendances as fans would prefer to invest in a season ticket for the real spectacle rather than one coming at them through a 24 inch screen. Ironically, the spiralling cost of attending football in the 90s outweighs the cost of buying a satellite dish which has the benefits of numerous services and will eventually pay for itself after several years. It could be argued that the income earned by the Premier League clubs from pay-to-view should go to keeping the price of attending football down.

The FSA has persistently urged some form of appreciation from the clubs and the football authorities for the fans' role in making live games a TV spectacle. The deals struck up between the football authorities and television have not been seen as 'fan friendly'. As

Nigel Grant argued in the FSA newsletter in February 1991:

> When the deals are re-negotiated, the FSA must ensure that, however much the authorities demand from TV, they must be reminded of their obligation to take account of the interests of the people who put considerably greater amounts of money into the game than television, namely us, the supporters (*Football Supporter*, Issue 13).

This plea for some form of consultation between fans, the football authorities and television came in the wake of BSkyB's decision to stage a 3rd. Round FA Cup tie between Manchester United and QPR on a Monday night, in January 1991. The movement of FA Cup ties has set a precedent for the movement of Premier League games, and the manner in which both decisions ride roughshod over the interests of the fans has been heavily criticized by the FSA and fanzines alike. The 3rd. Round cup tie at Old Trafford only managed to attract an attendance of 36,065 where two years previously the same fixture drew a crowd of 46,257. Such figures were seen as evidence by many outraged fans that their worst fears had been realized, of fans being deterred from going to football because of the rescheduling of games to awkward days and times. Dave Colwell in the general football fanzine *A Novel School of Thought* (Issue 1) sarcastically lampooned QPR fans who had the unenviable task of travelling up to Manchester on a Monday night arguing: "Come on you R's fans you'll be back in Euston at 5.21 am on the Tuesday morning, in plenty of time to get to work."

Chairman of Manchester United, Martin Edwards, had spoken out about the rescheduling of the tie but it was perceived as a laughable retort to the FA by many fans who consider Edwards' ambitions towards superleague status as a reason for negotiations with television. United fans were further aggrieved later on in the competition when the 5th. Round cup tie was again rescheduled for a Monday night; this time at Norwich. Fanzines again expressed their anger towards the satellite company, the FA and the club. The front cover of *United We Stand* (Issue 8) voiced its opinion in no uncertain terms with a banner superimposed among a crowd of fans, reading "Up Yours BSkyB!". Inside, the editorial ran:

If the game was on a Saturday United would have taken about 7-

8000 to East Anglia, but we will be lucky to take 3-4000. I for one will be missing my first game since last September when I was on holiday. It was not that I cannot make it to Norwich, (although it is difficult) or that I don't want to go, but I am not going as a matter of principle. Just who do BSkyB think they are? Moving games here and there to suit their tiny army of watchers. The FA shouldn't allow such deals to be made. I thought Fergie had a cheek in the *Evening News* by saying "It's a shame, but I just hope the fans can dig a little deeper into their pockets because we need their support". The cheeky sod. If United are that gutted about the decision then why don't they put on free coaches to loyal fans? It won't cost a fraction of the £60,000 they received for the game being televised.

Such vitriol for television's interference with the game is not uncommon among fanzines. The ushering in of Monday night games to cater for the new Premier League TV deal provoked similar outrage, for similar reasons. Aggrieved at the fact that fans are already being priced out of football at the turnstiles due to all-seater stadia, buying a dish is not an easily affordable option for many fans. In a letter to *The Guardian,* one fan wrote:

Buy a dish say BSkyB, but I wouldn't mind betting that by the time I shell out £250, the greedy men who appear to control sport these days will have shifted the whole thing to a channel where I have to pay a bit more (*The Guardian*, 23.5.92).

Another letter asked whether, with the inevitable extension of the footballing coverage from Saturday to Monday, *Match of the Day* would be renamed *Match of the Weekend*. Ironically, fanzine writers and readers have often expressed their support for the return of recorded highlights on a Saturday night in the format of the old *Match of the Day*. In February 1990, *When Saturday Comes* conducted a survey which attempted to gauge opinion on ITV's *The Match* and preferable alternatives. Only 18% were happy with ITV's format of live Sunday games, while 75% voted for a return of a *Match of the Day* type of programme (*WSC*, May 1990). *WSC* had continually voiced its dissatisfaction with *The Match*, due to the programmes' over-exposure of 'The Big Five'. In July 1989 the *WSC* editorial argued that such selective coverage leads to fans only identifying with a small percentage of clubs and players, which affects the long term access for new generations of football fans. Televised football offered a number of shared references to readers of *WSC* and other fanzines, and was "being eroded away". Yet the *WSC* survey is problematic, as the figures for *The Match* highlight the programme's popularity. It is the contradictory nature of televised football's audience that undermines the claims of the football fan lobby as voiced through the FSA and the fanzines.

The uphill task of taking on the media industries has not dissuaded fans from voicing their discontent and humour to be derived from the televised game. Many members of the FSA resent the fact that more young fans follow teams shown on TV rather than local sides which have traditionally nurtured young people's interest in the game. In one of three articles by FSA members under the heading "Tunnel Vision?", Peter Wakefield bemoaned the features of the game that are lost in TV coverage of the major clubs, or as he put it "the first, the fashionable, and the famous". While acknowledging the fact that TV gave access to the likes of Pele, Eusabio, Platini, and Maradona, he would still plump for "the smell of grass, mud, liniment, sweat, Oxo, tobacco, rain and boredom". Finally he argued:

> With all its risks and discomforts I still prefer the real thing, followed by the piece of football broadcasting that remains beyond criticism - the only magic litany of grief, joy and indifference that is James Alexander Gordon and the Classified Results. Now there's a good name for a band! (*Reclaim The Game*; November/December 1989).

Such laments for the 'terrace experience' - in this case the dulcet tones of a BBC Radio sports reporter - are commonplace among fanzine articles, many juxtaposing the experience of attending a game and sitting in an armchair watching the 'footy on the telly'. Demonstrating that the football experience is totally about context and the environment within which it is watched, Harry Pearson (*WSC*, January 1989) provided a guide on how to create an "authentic matchday atmosphere" while watching *The Match*. The numerous recommendations included: opening doors and windows; placing a length of railing in front of the screen; being searched before entering the living room, and putting on "a Sisley sweatshirt, Pepe jeans, Timberland loafers and half a pint of hair gel"; then finally, switching off the TV five minutes from time to avoid the rush! This is not only a humorous antidote to sterile TV viewing, but also a social comment on the discomforts of actually going to the match. Other fanzine articles reflect the agony of not actually being there and having to suffer 90 minutes of pure hell screaming at the TV set. The May/June 1992 edition of *The Absolute Game* carried a cartoon that reflected the feelings of many Scots, used to their country's humiliation at International tournaments, prior to the 1992 European Championships. Sat in an armchair anticipating the worst, the character, clad in Scotland shirt, is smoking a gamut of 'ciggies' while at his feet lies a 6 pack of valium, a straight-jacket and a leaflet from the Samaritans. Such humour is an overt and inventive expression of the multiplicity of meanings viewers can produce from watching football on TV.

As argued earlier the popularity of some football programmes on TV belies the crassness of the shows themselves. However, TV programmes are 'producerly texts' (Fiske, 1989) which escape the control of preferred meanings of TV producers creating a polysemy of meaning. This helps to explain the contradictory nature of the popularity of ITV's *Saint and Greavsie* or BBC's Jimmy Hill and John Motson. Parodying the success of such media icons, fanzines play with the 'tele-expert' commentaries on the game, highlighting through humour exactly where such programmes fail to meet the fans expectations. For example: *Off The Ball* , whose title itself plunders Brian Moore's old ITV programme *On The Ball* , produced a list of the "Ten Worst Soccer TV Pundits"; *Attack* (September 1990) who carried a cartoon strip "Vain and Greabo - the crap TV duo!"; and *The Abbey Rabbit* had a feature in each issue entitled "John Motson's Very Interesting Football Facts" referring to the commentator's never ending inane ramblings on football facts and figures. There are many more articles, cartoons and humorous anecdotes which express similar disdain for the way football is presented on TV.

It is not only football programmes which come under attack but also the portrayal of football fans in other contexts on TV. For example, ITV's drama series *The Bill* had a storyline about the undercover policing of fans which was taken apart by the Sunderland fanzine *Wise Men Say* (No. 8). The programme was considered to have shown a complete lack of authenticity, with clichéd accounts of covert police operations. Moreover, it was argued that a major reason for broadcasting such an episode was the topicality of policing football due to The Football Spectators' Bill passing through Parliament at the time of screening. Under the heading "Bill Of Wrongs" the fanzine suggested:

> Taking it at face value, the script seemed to have been written by Colin Moynihan under the influence of repeated showings of West Side Story (*Wise Men Say*, No. 8, 1989).

There have been attempts to produce more serious and informed pieces of drama and documentary about football in recent years: *The Manageress* (C4, 1989); *The Firm* (ITV, 1989); *Shooting Stars* (C4,1990); *United* (BBC 2, 1990); *Video Diaries - Italia 90, Bobby's Army* (C4,1991); *Standing Room Only* (BBC 2, 1991); and numerous news/current affairs programmes have had 'fan friendly' reports on football such as *Reportage* (BBC 2), *On The Line* (BBC 2), and *World In Action* (ITV). The Video Diaries of Kevin Allen's jaunt at Italia '90 was a two hour programme that attempted to capture the essence of being an England fan in Sardinia, reflecting the problems that fans encounter on such excursions and conveying both the lighter and more harrowing moments of such a tour. The 'amateurish' video footage helped to convey an authenticity usually lacking in more conventional documentaries and offered a set of alternative narratives to the stereotypical portrayal of English fans by the press. A later attempt to develop and communicate a 'fan friendly' perspective in the media was *Standing Room Only*, a form of TV fanzine produced under the umbrella of Janet Street Porter's Def II, on BBC 2. Fronted by Simon O'Brien, previously of the soap Brookside, the programme received an indifferent response from fanzine editors but has proved to be popular as a third series is now being planned.

The exploration in other media forms by fans, apart from the printed fanzine, is something that has been recommended by, among others, Adrian Goldberg (previous editor of *Off The Ball*). Such an argument brings us back into the possibilities and difficulties arising from developments in satellite and cable TV, along with the boom in portable video production for the 'home entertainment' market. Just as fans found the possibilities afforded by the developments in personal computers to make inroads into the publishing media, so the developments in audio-visual equipment enable the possibility of entering into broadcast media. There appear to be two processes taking place, simultaneously growing out of technological and socioeconomic changes. The globalization of the media and the creation of a "European audio-visual space" (Robin and Cornford, *Marxism Today*, November 1991), and localization, where new broadcasting spaces are possible where previously there were none, especially in Britain which has had to endure a duopoly of TV broadcasting by the BBC and ITV companies. Channel 5, which will be the last new terrestrial station in Britain, as proposed in the 1990 Broadcasting Act, may create and stimulate local programme producers, necessary to sustain a regional media industry. The rationale behind such ventures would be to encourage local development and inward investment. Many fans, especially of smaller League clubs, bemoan the scant coverage their teams receive on television. The possible local emphasis of Channel 5 could, given necessary motivation and planning, provide a platform for in-depth coverage of local teams and football programmes that cater for local tastes. However, as Robin and Cornford have suggested:

> In the absence of a meaningful decentralisation of power in our society, local media could simply become a distraction, creating the illusion of community rather than playing a part in its renewal. The danger is that they simply become a symbolic gesture to some long-lost ideal of community (*Marxism Today*, Nov. 1991).

Maybe cable networks could offer greater possibilities in the long-term, where fans could produce their own programmes/videos to be aired on an open-access channel? For the meantime, in the knowledge that advertisers - the major customers of TV - hold the power with regards to policy, logistics of transmission and production of programmes, fans will continue to subvert the proffered meanings of the global media industry.

8　The lad done brilliant: Football writing, consumption and identity

I have met women who have loved football, and go to watch a number of games a season, but I have not yet met one who would make that Wednesday night trip to Plymouth. And I have met women who love music, and can tell their Mavis Staples from their Shirley Browns, but I have never met a woman with a huge and ever-expanding and neurotically alphabetised record collection .... I am not saying that the anally retentive woman does not exist, but she is vastly outnumbered by her masculine equivalent (Nick Hornby, 1992, p.103).

The disparity between men and women in their level of obsessiveness for football which Nick Hornby attempts to convey in the above passage, taken from his best-selling autobiography *Fever Pitch*, reflects and reiterates an apparent subjective difference between the sexes when it comes to football, indeed any sport. Throughout *Fever Pitch* football is constantly used as a metaphor for Hornby's life, and in several instances, Hornby's life appears as a metaphor for the ups and downs of his beloved Arsenal. The two appear inseparable and the book, more than anything, illustrates the processes by which football is a constant in the life of many men. That is, a constant narrative of cup runs, relegation battles and Championship races. Moreover, for many men, as life appears to drift along with the occasional significant event, the hopes and fears embodied in supporting a football team somehow fill the gaps. To his credit Hornby self-reflectively extracts the contradictory nature in which football, at varying times, inflicts a certain paralysis over other aspects of his life (education, career, relationships). As he self-consciously and ironically confesses, "that is what football has done to me. It has turned me into someone who would not help if my girlfriend went into labour at an impossible moment" (ibid. p.106).

Hornby is surely not alone in his account of an obsession with football. But how and why does football become so central to a large section of the male population? And for those girls and women who also enjoy playing and watching the game, how and why is their position within the football configuration continually challenged, suppressed, or castigated?

The aim of this chapter is to textually and sociologically analyse the manner in which football is constitutive of male identity, and alternatively, to analyse attempts to challenge the discursive reproduction of the masculine ideal in both playing and watching the game, and through football, into wider social domains. In many respects, therefore, this chapter underpins the analytic theme of the whole book: the processes by which football, as it is both lived and mediated, structures and is structured by male pleasures. Firstly, the chapter will map out theoretical developments in the analysis of gender and popular culture relevant to the study of football fanzines; secondly, analyse the place of fanzines and the 'new football man' within male football consumption and identity; and thirdly, highlight specific challenges to male practice and discourse in fanzines and the ever expanding domain of football.

Sport, textual politics and men's genres

Football's popularity amongst men has been bound by its reportage - literary, verbal, and visual - within the mass media. This male 'sports chatter', referred to by Umberto Eco (1986), covers large amounts of time or space within newspaper columns, magazine articles, radio features and television programmes yet has, in Britain, been largely under theorized, specifically with regard to print media. With the exception of Rowe (1991) the 'naturalization' of the affinity between the world of sports writing and its mode of address to a male audience has been theoretically ignored. However, studies of magazines targeted at a female audience have been analysed at length, most notably by Angela McRobbie (1982), Janice Winship (1987, p.1991), and Helen Pleasance (1991).

In the analysis of other fields of popular entertainment - literature, film and television - there has been a theoretical feminization of mass consumption. For instance, studies of women's genres in film (melodrama) and television (soap opera) emphasize the 'construction of narratives motivated by female desire and processes of spectator identification governed by female point-of-view' (Kuhn, 1984, p.18). Moreover, soap operas offer an open-ended narrative and the flow of daytime television a 'distracted' gaze of the viewer which corresponds with the rhythms and demands of women's work in the home (Modleski, 1983). The above research on feminine subject positions, across the different forms of mass media, stress a common concern in assessing the progressive or transformative potential of women's genres. Sadly, the progressive and transformative potential of men's genres has been neglected. Unlike the feminist challenge to the traditional view of women's genres as generating passive forms of consumption, the 'classical' model of male genres views mediated sport as linear, goal orientated and fetishistic. One reason for the lack of analytical or political challenges to such an omnipresent discourse is that 'realism' forms a feature of dominant media representations of sport. The processes of signification in such representations of sport are grounded on the assumption that meanings exist already in society and that they 'operate as neutral vehicles for conveying those meanings from source to recipient' (Kuhn, 1993, p.156). Therefore, sport, and specifically football, is signified as a 'natural' male domain.

The schematic split between the media genres of soap opera and sport have most recently been theorized as having similarities in their modes of address, albeit to distinct popular audiences divided along gender lines. Exploratory papers by Rose and Friedman (1992) and O'Connor and Boyle (1993) both dissent from popular conceptions of masculine forms of mass entertainment. In their analysis of televised sport both studies argue that such programmes mirror the structure and reception of soap opera in that they are: (1) open-ended, cyclical and melodramatic in textual structure, invoking emotional identification; (2) reflective of a distracted experience of reception related to domestic life and leisure; and (3) explicitly addressed to male audiences attempting to re-affirm gender identities. These studies illustrate that the political economy and aesthetic structure of the mass media are gendered, targeted as distinct male and female markets. With this knowledge in mind, it is possible to provide an applied textual reading of football writing and fanzines as subgenres of masculine forms of media representation.

Football, consumption and masculinity

Joyce Layland has pointed to the latent effect of seeing feminist research as exclusively about women's lives; the very fact that men's lives often go unquestioned; and that what is left is, inevitably, 'male as norm'. What Layland calls for is a demystification of power and its components, the major culprit in feminist discourse being the production of 'masculinity' and 'masculine behaviour'. She contends that, "the production of 'masculinity' or 'femininity' is in part, the result of individuals being presented with different sets of possibilities of how to make sense of a given situation" (1990, p.129). Moving from literary to cultural studies feminist analysis of women's magazines enlighten and inform any attempt at forming a critique of masculine texts or publications which address a male readership and how men relate to such texts.

A dominant theme running through many feminist studies of popular magazines has been the 'open' and 'closed' nature of the text. Closure within the text suggests the successful establishment of hegemonic relations of class, gender and race, where a popular cultural form seeks t o re-affirm dominant social positions. For instance, Pleasance's (1991) study of women's magazines highlights how feminine identity is fixed in magazines through particular representations of consumption. Gendered narratives of consumption, appearing to offer choice and freedom, in fact hide the lack of material choice open to many women. The flip side of this gendered narrative of consumption is epitomized in the new men's magazines which have blossomed since the 1980s with the emergence of *FHM* (1982, circulation: 60,000), *Arena* (1986, circulation: 80,000), *GQ* (1988, circulation: 80,000), and *Esquire* (1991, circulation: 65,000). Collier (1991) and Winship (1987) both argue that such publications have not met with unqualified success. In an attempt to develop non-sexist ideology, the magazines still push products for men with an emphasis on power, money, business and sporting success: invariably dodging the issue of male sexuality. As Winship concludes of the difference between men's and women's magazines:

Our lives as women and men continue to be culturally defined in materially different ways, and both what we read and how it is presented to us reflects, and is part of, that difference (1987, p.6).

Nowhere is this distinction more starkly realized than in the highly gendered consumption of football texts, products and performances by men. This is not to suggest that women do not participate in football subculture, but that consumption of football related goods and services is connoted as a masculinized ritual, and that while on the periphery, women are all but excluded from such patterns of conspicuous consumption.

The targeting of football ephemera has its historical antecedents which led to specific forms of gender exclusion. For instance: the nineteenth century sporting press (see Mason, 1980); the match programme which began in the late nineteenth century (see Shaw, 1980); the club newsletter or magazine such as *Watford* (Watford FC) which from being established in 1891 when the club was founded continues today; and finally, cigarette cards of football players which helped spawn a whole new masculine pastime of 'cartophily' (the collection of cigarette cards). Indeed, cigarette cards like *Will's Famous Footballers*, *Hill's Football Club Captain's*, *Player's Association Cup Winners*, and *Taddy's Prominent Footballers* all appeared before the First World War, with Taddy's collection containing over 800 cards. Tobacco cards had first emerged in the 1880s carrying pictures of 'beautiful women' or 'famous actresses' and were addressed to a male consumer, specifically towards the army, and football at the turn of the century was merely the next subject to be used as a marketing ploy to attract the male smoking public.

Post-war magazines and books began to appear as the boom years of British football seemed to grip the whole country. This saw the emergence of magazines like *Football Monthly* in 1951 (which still has a modest circulation of 12,000) and the publication of autobiographies by famous footballers like the later Billy Wright of Wolves and England whose book *The World's My Football Pitch* (published by Arrow Books in paperback) sold in excess of sixty five thousand copies. But the main tug on male purse strings came in the 1960s, IPC Magazines Ltd launching two football titles either end of the decade and targeted at different age groups: *World Soccer* (1961) aimed at the adult market and *Shoot* (1969) aimed at teenagers (the latter currently enjoying a weekly circulation in excess of 140,000).

117

With the recent boom in football merchandising IPC Magazines have more recently launched two further football magazines: *Soccer Stars* (1992), targeted at boys in the 11-17 age range with a circulation of over 90,000, and *90 Minutes* (1990) targeted at men aged 18-35 with a circulation of over 65,000. However, the first major turning point in the transformation of football memorabilia arrived with the staging of the World Cup in England in 1966. As Phil Shaw has noted:

> The commercial explosion which accompanied the World Cup in England made many people in the game sit up and realise that there was an enormous market for well-designed, attractive merchandise. That year millions of key-rings, mugs, ashtrays and books portraying the tournament's mascot, a lion called 'World Cup Willie' were sold to a public that was beginning to rediscover its passion for Britain's national game (Shaw, 1980, p.8).

Football bubble gum cards and later the Panini football sticker album series, which have been promoted on a large scale since 1976, created a whole new playground subculture as young boys gathered to barter and swap in order to capture the elusive card or sticker to complete their collection. Of course, certain would be withheld from sale until later in the season so that boys amassed packs of duplicates, thus increasing the 'cultural capital' of a rare card or sticker. Moreover, fans could delight in the relentless publication of football annuals (many compiled by national newspapers), inane biographies and books to improve soccer skills.

These publications carried a mode of address which constructed narratives motivated by male desires. An example is the continuing link between football and tobacco companies with the *Park Drive Book of Football* series published from the mid 60s to the mid 70s. These books celebrated the masculine imaginary of football helping to fuel young male appetites for the game and reproduce divisive dominant discourses. By employing high profile players and managers of the day (for example, Derek Dougan of Wolves or Don Review of Leeds) or celebrities from other areas of popular entertainment (like Liverpool comedy performer Ken Dodd) the series invoked emotional identification with the masculine football spectacle. For instance, Derek Dougan's account of the 'modern' game in the 1970 edition entitled 'Football is a Man's Game' epitomized the philosophy which kept the sport a male preserve, the title itself an immediate give-away as to whose game it was. Opening up his argument about the significant changes that had taken place within the game during the latter stages of the sixties Dougan pronounced:

Emancipation is one thing: a man's sport another - professional football is a man's game. If by the term we mean physically exacting and tough on the muscles. I don't know what the game was like when the Football League was founded. Life in those days was tough to the point of being grim. People were used to hardship, but I doubt if footballers had the sinews and the capacity for endurance that are needed and demanded today (1970, p.109).

He continued:

To say that football is 'a man's game' does not imply that it is ruthless, brutal and insensitive. It means that skill has to be forged on an anvil of physical endurance. And they say a woman's work is never done! (1970, p.109).

These two brief passages (the rest of the article continues in similar vein) are loaded with metaphors of masculine dominance (circumscribed by references to bodily superiority: 'physically exacting', 'sinews', and 'endurance') and feminine weakness based on a 'naturalization' of the divide between the women's political struggle for 'emancipation' in public domains and the masculine domain of sport. This discursive split provides further ideological weight invested in the view that the 'weak' female body is directly responsible for women's position in society. Dougan's language is typical of that produced within football literature and reportage from the earliest representations of the game. All this is in spite of his insistence on the difference between 'modern' football and the game in 'those days' when life 'was tough to the point of being grim'. Even this analogy is gendered by the suggestion that the 'modern' man's game utilizes skill, connoting sensitivity with the ball (the feminine), but in a subservient relationship with muscular power ('forged on an anvil of physical endurance').

The above history of football texts and reception illustrates how dominant masculine discourses have continuously constructed the game's culture and, how discourses on football construct gendered bodies. But do they continue to have a dominant position within contemporary representations of football? Football fanzines and the 'new football writing' have challenged sports journalism practice, but has this subjective change in representations of the game transformed the gender specificity of previous modes of address? Fanzines represent a written manifestation of 'sports chatter', their content possessing similarities with male conversations to be heard in the public domains of the workplace and the pub. However, the form and content of this discourse and its meaning to its participants has changed over time, masculinity in the post-punk era producing new meanings around football. With changes in men's conspicuous consumption in the 1980s, football as popular culture is a space of intertextuality. The most visual sign of the new culture has been the sartorial changes introduced by young men at football. As Redhead has argued about the fashion consciousness of football fans:

> Soccer in Britain, for a century the opiate of the working man, is a surprising location for designer menswear and its specific connotation of a crisis in masculinity (*New Socialist*, 1987, No. 47).

Frank Mort has also documented the changing surfaces of male youth as they make their way to the turnstiles in the mid 80s:

> Individuality is on offer, incited through commodities and consumer display. From jeans: red tabs, designer labels, distressed denim. To hair: wedges, spiked with gel, or pretty boys who wear it long, set off with a large earring. And the snatches of boys talk I pick up are about 'looking wicked' as well as the game. Which is not to say the violence is designer label (Mort, 1988, p.193).

Redhead picks up on this latter point suggesting that the 'skin-deep body politics of football chic' in the 1980s and early 90s have still seen the affirmation and reassertion of traditional masculine styles in the reign of the Tory government. As Janice Winship neatly puts it: "under many a new man fashion look lurks a diehard wolf" (1987, p.153). The 'New Man' has given way to another media fiction the 'New Lad' who may be sympathetic to feminist aspirations but has no scruples when it comes to picking up a copy of the *Sunday Sport*. For Neville Wakefield (1990) the smile that crosses the faces of those who read the *Sunday Sport* belongs to an "intertextual space which, in shedding its mortgage to the real, appeals to the sort of ironic sense of play" and "a newly invigorated sense of the comic" (1990, p.15). This intertextuality where cultural practices are produced through the interconnection of a range of texts, and the "newly invigorated sense of the comic" is central to the success of football fanzines and prevalent in football subculture as a whole. Football is also central to the typology of the 'New Lad' as David Singh in the magazine *Deadline* (February 1994) outlined in the following 'identikit picture':

> The New Lad has had a bellyful of the bleating about the brutal and over-competitive nature of sports. Much as CAMRA gave beer drinkers a sort of licence to regard their pastime as a high cultural pursuit on a par with oil painting or classical music appreciation, so *When Saturday Comes* and Nick Hornby's *Fever Pitch* have given him a licence to regard football as gruff savage ballet or metaphor for the comedie humaine.

This supposedly new masculine subjectivity is clearly reminiscent of traditional discourses that I illustrated earlier. Despite being cited as one area of political contestation within sport, in terms of gender politics, fanzines are invariably edited, written and read by men. A case in point is the much lauded magazine *When Saturday Comes*. Their target audience is men aged 18-35, in the ABC socioeconomic groups, who grew up watching football in the late 60s and early 70s, the era characterized as the birth of the 'modern' professional game. The masculine mode of address invokes similar structures of feeling and sensibility between text and reader by employing emotional identification with specific cultural references. For instance, humour is often derived from masculine genres within television, fashion or music from the 60s and 70s, references that conjure up nostalgia for past stars and teams, and boyhood football dreams from kicking a football in a back alley to playing on Wembley's 'sacred' turf. While not openly sexist, male subjectivity is inscribed within the *WSC* text, and football fanzines in general, offering a subtle brand of male bonding. One glimpse at the names on the letters page gives the male game away! Ironically, fanzines offer another all male line-up in keeping, rather than in contrast, to the predominantly male football tele-experts and press reporters. Further, according to a survey of female football supporters by Jackie Woodhouse (1991) for the Sir Norman Chester Centre for Football Research, the media image of football, as masculine and 'war like', was given as the area most in need of change. In arguing that women fans and players have a genuine interest and knowledge of football Woodhouse states:

Female writers are able to offer an alternative perspective on the game and provide an important vehicle for the articulation of the views of female fans. Equally as important, by gaining respect and recognition through writing about the game in a knowledgeable and entertaining fashion, such women can play a key role in challenging the macho attitudes and image of British football (Woodhouse, 1991, p.48).

The agenda now turns to the effacement of the dominant (masculine) signification processes within representations of football. If fanzines and the 'new football writing' can challenge and subvert traditional modes of sports writing, is there a space for challenging male hegemonic practices in football, and further, what new sporting practices would emerge from such textual politics?

Football with(out) balls

There appears two processes by which gender politics can produce transformation in football texts and social practice: one grounded in the deconstruction of dominant representations of sport; and a second grounded on a form of sports writing and experience marked as more 'other' to dominant male subjectivity: as a 'feminine' mode of sports representation and praxis.

The process of deconstruction aims to provoke the spectators awareness of the actual existence and effectivity of dominant codes of mediated sport, and consequently to engender a critical attitude towards these codes. For instance, the textual operations and modes of address which characterize dominant sports writing become the actual object of deconstructive football writing, opening up a space for active intervention and questioning on the part of readers in the meaning production process. Parody of dominant codes causes a distanciation between the reader and text, evoking a critical attitude by the fan to a particular element or form of sports writing.

Parody of football culture as a whole can also produce a similar distanciation by both football lovers and people without any specific affinity for the game. An example of this form of deconstructive process occurred amongst the media hype for the World Cup in Italia '90. Fashion in football was turned on its head to football in fashion as John Galliano, one of Italy's top designers, sent out the world's top models wearing customized Umbro football shirts, paired with striped trousers. In an article by *The Independent*'s fashion writer, Roger Tredre, entitled 'Designer stripes on the ball - The World Cup has kick started soccer style for women', designer Helen Storey was said to have taken up the football theme for her Autumn '90 collection. In true fashion writer style Tredre commented on Storey:

> Not content with customising soccer shirts, she has developed a complete 'football for women' look. She has designed high-cut soccer shorts with beads around the thighs and turned footballs into hip-bags. For evening, she has come up with striped satin hooded bomber jackets and evening dresses with players numbers on the back (*The Independent*, June 1990).

Further, Storey defended her tongue in cheek intervention into football subculture by stating, "Football is a very male-dominated game. I liked the idea of the swapping of roles, making football clothing sexy." The humorous parody of football within the hyperreal context of 'high couture' produces an open-ended representation of the game, allowing contradictory readings which can alert the spectator to the fictional aspects of both football and fashion.

Other fantastical representations of football culture have occurred within cinema and television drama. Bill Forsyth's film *Gregory's Girl* and Stan Hey's TV drama *The Manageress* both provide fictional challenges to dominant representations of women in football. In *The Manageress*, Cheri Lunghi stars as a female football manager who changes the fortunes of a professional football club. Lunghi's character is made credible because of her upbringing by an ex-pro player (her father), providing her with a superior knowledge of the game. However, Hey's narrative of the football wise female in a 'man's world' is undermined by recourse to stereotypical feminine modes of address as 'the manageress' has to choose between a career or her family life. In the interplay between masculine and feminine subject positions (a combination of mastery and masochism) there is continual recourse to the repressed role of mother and wife. While

The Manageress may have raised the possibility of female desire from the female point of view, its oppositional potential has to be placed in the context of the programme's reception. Cynical statements abounded about the unlikely event of a woman managing a professional football club. Few male players in the game took the idea seriously, which was epitomized by Gary Lineker, the previous darling of English football, who when asked if he could envisage working with a female football manager replied: "I could if she looked like that" referring to the actress Cheri Lunghi. Deconstructive challenges to the dominance of male subjectivity in representations of football have fallen short of materially transforming the gender divisions in the game as it is lived and it is because of these inadequacies that we now turn to more successful attempts by feminist discourses within the domain of sport to transform the game of football.

The majority of studies on football which have tried to theorize about the game, have often oversimplified the many variants that have made it such a popular sport amongst men. Much has been written about football and its relation to class, but there has often been neglect of the 'unseen' or 'unheard' discourse of gender and sexuality (along with ethnicity). The earliest forms of sports feminism grew out of the desire for equality of opportunity with men, and its liberal attributes were essentially pragmatic. The Women's Football Association has campaigned along the lines of equal opportunities, with the incentive for women to get into a traditional male sport. While not to ignore such a positive strategy as influential in encouraging more women to play football, recent socialist feminist perspectives on sport would argue that it fails to offer any radical alternatives. Women's football involves an element of 'separatism', which as Jennifer Hargreaves (1990) points out is an ideology that intends to "give women access to the most masculinized sports, create wider experiences to administer and control their own activities." Yet such an ideology threatens to exclude not only men but women too. Again, Hargreaves argues such unnecessary divisions neglect "to look at ways in which women and men are exploited **together** in sport and how relations articulate with capitalist relations" (1990, p.295). Following on from this argument Hargreaves suggests three strategies for change in female sport:

1. Co-option into a male sphere of activity.

2. A separatist all female strategy.
3. A cooperative venture with men for qualitative new models in which differences in the sexes are unimportant.

These strategies, specifically the third, are of vital importance to understanding the way in which male identity is constituted in football. The problem for both men and women who challenge dominant myths of male supremacy in sport is that such attempts produce stronger forms of male bonding. Cynthia Cockburn highlights these ironies when she says:

Since male power is not merely ideological but also based in wealth, social organization and physical might, femininity has had little power of its own to force adaptions in its complementary oppressor. The initiative normally lies with masculinity. That is what is so startling about feminism, and why our project so often seems unlikely to succeed (1988, p.321).

Even where women show an interest in football it often has to be legitimated or mediated through husbands or boyfriends. For instance, in one of his anecdotes about life, love and football, Nick Hornby explains how men believe that they understand the game far more implicitly than women, as if men were born with a natural capacity for interpreting the game. He goes on to describe a series of events which led him to vociferously challenge the right of his girlfriend to *feel* as strongly about Arsenal as he did. He concludes the tale by explaining that once he had shouted 'You don't understand' there was no turning back, and he could 'safely and smugly say' that he was 'top Arsenal dog in this house,' and that if they had children it would be his 'bottom exclusively that fills our season-ticket seat' (1992, p.174).

Female fans have challenged these 'naturalized' beliefs that men have a right to support a club over and above women's desires. A women's football fanzine *Born Kicking* represents one such challenge, by reporting on women's involvement in the game as both fans and players. As a passionate believer in the women's game Jane Purdon, the editor, launched the fanzine at a crucial time in the game's development towards the end of 1990. The main objectives of the fanzine were fourfold:

1. To publicize women's teams and leagues, helping women who want to play find teams and coaching.

2. To give support to and report on the national teams.
3. To provide a forum for women whose main interest is not as players but as spectators, giving a valuable contribution to current debates on football in this country.
4. To campaign where possible, from pushing for a national women's league to the provision of tampon machines at football grounds.

Despite sporadic appearances on the fanzine racks within Sportspages and independent record stores up and down the country, *Born Kicking* provides a welcome instance of cultural contestation to masculine representations of football.

Another innovative idea to highlight the position of women within the football subculture was an event entitled *Blowing the Whistle* an electronic animation which paid tribute to female endeavour in football. Commissioned and presented by Moviola, a Liverpool based multimedia arts group, and Oldham Art Gallery, the animation inspired by a Victorian photograph of a woman pegging out 12 football jerseys on a washing line, was shown simultaneously at Goodison Park (Everton) and Boundary Park (Oldham Athletic). Recognising the supportive roles women play in football, the press release for the event read:

> *Blowing the Whistle* shows that football really is a funny old game, and most definitely a game of two halves - men and women. The 15 second animation see gyrating washing machines, steaming irons and jostling team shirts triumphantly parading across the screen. Interspersed with statistics on women and football, it aims to symbolize what every wife, mother or girlfriend knows; that without them the game would never have gotten off the ground.

These ventures are visible attempts to challenge male identity head on, highlighting the fact that gender identity is not fixed. Therefore, this suggests that there are no continuous positions for men and women to achieve.

This argument leads, finally, to the issue of sexuality in football. Issues concerning homophobia, homosexuality and homoerotica bring to light some of the contradictions within representations of football and its consumption by men. Both men and women in sport face a contradictory array of heterosexual imperatives and homosexual possibilities. It is these tensions that produce images of the effeminate man or the mannish lesbian in dominant representations of sport. For although media sport addresses the audience as male, providing a continuously evolving world where spectatorship depends on identification, nearness and participation, the classical masculine pleasures in voyeurism and objectification can also produce a homoerotic gaze, where men watching men ironically subverts the conventional mode of sports viewing.

The codes and conventions of contemporary sports spectatorship can be traced back to Victorian ideals in sport, founded on the discourse of 'muscular manliness'. Organized sport, including Association Football, was greatly influenced by the rational recreations and the public school ethos of 'schooling the body' during the nineteenth century (see Bailey, 1978). Embodied in the construction of organized sport was the discourse of manliness associated with Muscular Christianity. As John Hargreaves has pointed out this 'cult of athleticism' had the desired effect of 'disciplining' or 'normalizing' the male youth of the 'dominant classes' (p.4). The strenuous activity of sport making it less likely that boys would indulge in 'indecent' behaviour. Muscular Christianity was influenced by evolutionary theory, the triumph of mind over body, but where 'the first requisite of life is to be a good animal' (Hargreaves, 1986, p.41). As the game of football was appropriated by the working class in the late nineteenth century, it is not surprising many of the newly organized League clubs had their origins in the church. The purpose of highlighting the roots of the modern game is to illustrate how the rational attempts to discipline the body and populations were, as Foucault has argued, responses to the urban crisis of this period, and that such disciplines have their parallels in contemporary society specifically within football. Football, as we have seen, still holds strong the virtues of manliness (aggression, physicality, competitive spirit and athletic skill), acting as a regulator of homosexuality amongst men, marginalizing it as 'perverse' or 'queer'. Eco (1986) in his polemical essay on football makes a cunning analogy when he likens his early encounters with the game to a 'terrified young homosexual' who forces himself to like girls. Eco describes why some boys do not get involved in football, invariably to receive the label of 'sissy' or 'puff':

I don't love soccer because soccer has never loved me, for from my earliest childhood I belonged to that category of infants or adolescents who, the moment they kick the ball - assuming that they manage to kick it - promptly send it into their own goal or, at best, pass it to the opponent, unless with stubborn tenacity they send it off the field, beyond hedges and fences, to become lost in a basement or a stream or to plunge among the flavours of the ice-cream cart. And so his playmates reject him and banish him from the happiest of competitive events (Eco, 1985, p.74).

Conversely to Eco's aversion to the game, homosexual men, being brought up as homosexual boys, accept that they are men like any other and often behave as such, which includes playing and watching football. As Metcalf argues:

Gay men are caught in the double bind of being told that we are not men yet being expected to behave as men (Metcalf, 1985, p.74).

However, the 1980s saw many homosexual men and women 'coming out' to affirm their gay or lesbian identity, a political act which was in direct opposition of the Thatcher government's moralistic tone. The spectre of AIDS created the 'pathologization of homosexuality' (Stacey, 1991, p.286), attacking the homosexual movement with charges of promiscuity and disease, claiming that they presented a risk to public health and morality. Section 28 encapsulated the attempt to sustain the institution of the nuclear family. The introduction of this homophobic legislation rather than silencing gay and lesbian voices, has subsequently put homosexuality high on the political agenda.

Football has been touched by the increased politicization of sexuality in the wake of Section 28. Justin Fashanu, one of Britain's earliest million pound signings, was the first footballer in this country to 'come out' and openly state his gay identity. This brave move, characteristically exploited on the pages of *The Sun*, prompted Andy Medhurst, a gay footballing fan, to write an article for *When Saturday Comes*. Promoting the erotic attractions of football Medhurst wrote:

Sport provides one of the few spaces in our anxious, repressed culture where one man can openly admire the body of another, as you'll find out by visiting any gym or standing on any terrace. This appreciation is, of course, heavily disguised and coded, but that doesn't make it less real (*WSC*, No. 47).

There now exists a Gay Football Supporters Network, said to be the largest special interest group by the magazine *Gay Times* (Redhead, 1991). Moreover, the football fanzine *The Football Pink* produced in Manchester is for gay and lesbian football supporters, the title itself a parody of that Saturday evening sports publication the *Pink 'Un*. The assertion of gay politics in football is a clear retort to the 'muscular masculinity' of the late nineteenth century, and offers further challenges to dominant representations of football. As Susan K. Cahn has argued about gay and lesbian sports people in general, footballers and spectators use:

... the social and psychic space of sport to create a collective culture and affirmative identity. Through traditionally masculine sporting traits of pride, competition and companionship (1993, p.364).

Football fanzines may have emerged out of the events at Heysel etc., attempting to challenge and transform the way the gamed is controlled and represented. But they have also enabled male producers and readers to redefine their ideas of masculinity when watching football. At a time of men's anxiety in relation to issues of sexuality, fanzines and the other means of contestation cited above, offer a way in which they can reveal or explain their social identities. This change to the postmodern, destroys traditional and modern football mythologies. There are no ready made identities to unproblematically take on, cultural differences yielding further openings and possibilities.

9 The absolute game: Football, racism and fascism in the New Europe

Mad dogs and Englishmen go out in the midday sun
Taking on the locals, every man jack of 'em
Stupid, drunken, gobby toughs
No excuse is good enough

Arrogant, ignorant, insensibly pissed
When you've nothing to prove, you prove it with your fists
This is England's chief export:
Football hooligans - an embarrassment to the sport.
(Sportchestra, *101 Songs About Sport*).

Diary of a racist

We have witnessed the unprecedented rise of independent football
fan literature, and documented noticeable shifts in the relationship
between those who run the game and those who watch it. It is,
therefore, ironic that the most popular publications charting the
everyday experiences of football fans have focused on football
related violence. Colin Ward's (1989) *Steaming In* and Bill Buford's
(1991) *Among The Thugs* provide biographical accounts of travelling
with English fans, at home and abroad, vividly portraying a sense of
camaraderie mixed with an intense chauvinism. Jay Allen's *Bloody
Casuals* is of a similar genre describing the exploits of Aberdeen
casuals in Scotland, but is not as widely available. The appearance of
these 'hooligan biographies' in the late 80s and early 90s could be
construed as signifying a resurgence of violent behaviour at football

131

or, at least, an acceptance that there are always going to be 'nutters' in the crowd wanting to cause trouble. Moreover, recent commentators, including John Williams, have suggested that 'football hooliganism' has a cyclical nature, and that we must be wary of its return.

The macabre fascination which society holds for violence is readily exploited by such biographical accounts which are marketed as 'eye-opening', revealing to 'us' the 'outsiders', cosseted from the supposedly frightening world of football supporters, exactly what takes place every Saturday in the side streets of city centres while the rest of us shop for our pleasure. Buford's use of narrative to describe his experiences 'among the thugs' - given in short, sharp, shocks - does capture the invigorated sense of pleasure certain individuals - Paraffin Pete and Daft Donald to name but two - obtain from crowd violence. Buford's American fascination with English youth cults had its antecedent with another North American, Richard Allen (a pen name of Jades Moffat originally from Canada), who wrote pulp fiction novels about skinheads in the early 70s. Allen's novels portrayed this particularly violent youth cult as both rough but noble. Like the 'hooligan biographies' of the past few years his books assumed that there is an inherent need for violence by groups of young men, frequently described in minute, graphic detail. The skinhead rears his shaven head in Buford's account of life on the terraces. Describing his induction onto the terraces he says:

> I entered the stands for the visiting supporters and ended up following a skinhead - big and brawny with a tight-fitting white T-shirt and fleshy biceps. His name, I would learn, was Cliff, which - sheer, unadorned, vaguely suggestive of danger - seemed entirely appropriate. The skinhead phase had long passed and even here, in this crowd, Cliff stood out as a nostalgic anomaly, but Cliff had such an aggressive manner - the regulation braces and the heavy black boots and pockets full of two pences (their edges sharpened beforehand) to throw at the Cambridge supporters - that he seemed the most obvious person to befriend (Buford, 1991, p.133).

A date is not provided for this particular encounter, but one must presume that it was sometime during the mid 80s. As most scholars of 'football hooliganism' are aware, the skins had a fleeting association with football yet still appear in the public imagination as the main protagonists of football violence. What came to symbolize the authentic 'reality' of the English male proletariat has now been exported as a symbol of the rising tide of nationalism across Europe, particularly in Germany. To complicate the picture even further the skinhead has now been caught up by the postmodern plundering of subcultural history by male homosexuals. This use of retro fashion has turned the aggressive masculinity of the boots, braces and tattoos into an ambiguous sexual fetish. Buford's account of a neo-Nazi birthday party in Bury St Edmonds, where skinheads work themselves up into a violent frenzy, not only appears isolated within his own book, but most importantly, from the contemporary milieu of football fandom in this country. His anecdotal evidence of football violence is outdated and often misleading, misrepresenting the broader composition of football supporters in the 1980s/90s. His compulsion for observing violence appears to be in league with the media's own morbid fascination with 'hooligans' and 'firms', heightening mythologies, creating the hyperreal sense that all football fans are violent. The effect of this media focus is captured by Williams (1991) when he says:

By the time the World Cup Finals were being staged in Italy, in 1990, 100 young Englishmen could, quite literally, became the centre of attention of the World's media, simply by parading drunkenly up the streets of Cagliari singing the national anthem. If you had been involved, the next day you could read about yourself on the front page of the English tabloids, which had been specially flown in to Sardinia for the occasion. This was fifteen minutes or more of instant fame (Williams, 1991, p.167).

The paradox of media and other written accounts of football violence in recent years is that they are being written - with admission by the authors - at a time when such 'aggro' is increasingly passé. The timing of Buford's book, after the positive virtues of Italia '90, the inflammatory nature of his accounts of violence and the bigoted fashion in which he patronizes the actual fans he encountered, are the three most annoying facets of *Among The Thugs*. The book rode on the crest of a football publishing wave engineered by the winds of change inspired by football fanzines.

The themes that Ward and Buford's treatise do vividly portray are

133

the racist and xenophobic character of many English fans. While the influence of the NF is often overstated in terms of football, despite Bulldog and other racist literature publishing a league of 'football hooligans' etc., in the 1980s racist abuse both domestically and abroad "remained a relatively routine feature of British football" (Williams, 1991, p.170). The fact that the majority of English clubs have black players on their books highlights the ambiguous and contradictory nature of racist abuse. As Williams (1991) has asserted, racism at football is a 'selective' operation, and he argues:

> ... working-class localistic, proprietorial pride can in certain circumstances constitute a form of ethnicism which resists, or subordinates, racism (e.g. when black football players represent your town, your club etc.) (Williams, 1991, p.170).

The most disturbing, and publicly discussed, domestic racist activity in football occurred when John Barnes and Mark Walters joined Liverpool and Rangers respectively in the mid-80s. Dave Hill's (1989) *Out Of His Skin* - the title an ironic parody of the football vernacular - documented what he termed 'the John Barnes phenomenon' focusing on the racist temperament of Liverpool's colonial past and footballing present. Hill, who has provided some of the most 'fanzinesque' football journalism on the pages of *The Independent On Sunday*, excavated not only the Jamaican roots of the successful black player but also the cultural roots of racism in British society. His suggestion that "Every visitor to Liverpool Football Club should inflict upon themselves the half-hour walk from Lime Street station to Anfield" (p63) is not only a reference to the racist graffiti which adorns this particular route, but also a warning of the sinister side of English pride which appears from the cracks of a once thriving industrial nation.

The success of black footballers in English football has caused a schism within the popular imagination of what their achievements in the sport signify. White football fans ambivalence to the spectacle of the black athlete, exemplified by the way John Barnes is adored domestically for Liverpool but vilified for his performances for England (surely his heart isn't in it?), can be traced to the mythological, culturally constructed matrix of power which endows black males with the stereotyped image of having a naturally muscular physique. This popular imagination that black footballers

134

are all brawn and no brains is deeply embedded and has only been demystified by the likes of Garth Crooks (previous chairman of the PFA and TV panelist) and John Fashanu (TV presenter and lucrative businessman). The ambiguity of white male hegemony has begun to raise a certain amount of consciousness to issues of racism on the terraces. The following excerpt from the fanzine *On The March* (Southampton) depicts the at times violent process of confronting the contradictions of idolizing what has come to be perceived as the 'racialised other':

> I lost my rag when one of the idiots started screaming 'Rodney Wallace is a wanker' and 'You black bastard Wallace'. Well in no hesitation I shouted over to him 'why don't you shut up and fuck off' which I think summed up everyones' feelings around me. Well this seemed to work, not too much heard from them for five minutes. Then, just what I was praying for happened, Wallace scored a goal and believe it or not this hypocrite was celebrating. Well I decided to ask him if Rodney was still 'a black bastard' now, things turned nasty and one of our lot was thrown out. The wanker then tried to reason with me, which understandably I refrained from. His mates claimed Saints supporters shouldn't fight each other, the thing was though, I didn't think anyone like that could support Saints. I just wondered what the young black woman behind me was thinking during all of this.

Mercer and Julien (1988) raise the point that black sportsmen are often 'idolized to the point of envy'. This recognizes the flip side of racist abuse in football, where statements like "our nigger is better than your nigger" are the most twisted and bizarre forms of bigoted allegiance.

Explicit political confrontation to sporadic, spontaneous and organized forms of racism have emerged out of the fanzine and independent football supporter's organizations. Leeds Fans United Against Racism and Fascism were the forerunners in the campaign to eradicate racism from the terraces. Responding to the racist literature peddled outside Elland Road, LFUARF published its own fanzine *Marching Altogether* which it distributes free of charge before matches. In a press release distributed to other fanzines LFUARF state:

For years at Leeds United the National Front have deliberately created a climate of racism for the purpose of furthering its fascist politics. With the backing of Leeds Trades Council, trades unions and a variety of groups LFUARF has turned the tide of racism at Elland Road and won national acclaim.

Other such organizations have appeared in Merseyside, the North East and most notably in Scotland where the Supporters Campaign Against Racism in Football (SCARF) started due to fears that fascist activity in Edinburgh appeared to be on the increase. Indeed, in the last general election the British National Party organized a campaign in the city, turning to the football terraces as recruitment grounds. SCARF, with the assistance of fanzines and the FSA, leafleted grounds highlighting 'The dangers of fascism' and the message to fans to 'TAKE A STAND TODAY - SHOUT DOWN THE RACIST'. The polemical stance taken by these campaigns has coincided with the re-emergence of the Anti-Nazi League in February 1992. The League had previously been integral to the late 70s/ early 80s cultural politics exemplified by Rock Against Racism who produced the fanzine *Temporary Hoarding* as its mouthpiece. However, these alliances which aimed to build subcultural politics around pop music were limited and ambiguous. Support for the bands associated with RAR often included those with a commitment to nationalism and fascist behaviour. Similar doubts about the possibilities of anti-racist football organizations have also surfaced. The fanzine *Our Day Will Come* (Manchester United/Glasgow Celtic) has argued for a more militant stance against racism in football suggesting:

> It's no use lobbying or pressurising directors, the League or the FA to start a preachy white liberal anti-racist campaign. It's a waste of our energy because these people and bodies are racist themselves, and because racism in the working class can only be tackled by the working class itself (*Our Day Will Come*, No. 10).

This 'liberal baiting' article offers a somewhat deterministic view of racism but does allude to its institutional nature. This institutional racism of football administrative bodies has caused a rift within the black football community itself. Garth Crooks and Brendon Batson have been tireless in their campaign to highlight racism in the game, but their anti-racist strategy frequently hides behind their allegiance to the football profession. The lack of any radical challenge to the broader implications football has in constructing racist and chauvinistic behaviour is due to the myopic belief that football 'can put its own house in order' born out of a history of insisting that sport should be distanced from politics. While the PFA do not wholeheartedly detract from the political stage, it is often left to black players like Howard Gayle (previously Blackburn Rovers) and non-league clubs like Almathak in Liverpool to prove that politics is personal - and that opposition to racism for them means having pride in their black identity.

Pressure to eliminate racial abuse within grounds did prompt Lord Justice Taylor to include among his recommendations a policy to arrest those who incite such behaviour. The inclusion of such a policy in the updated version of the government's Football Spectators Act 1989 does represent a positive step by the authorities to do something about racial discrimination, but has proved problematic to police, not least because of the difficulty in pinpointing the perpetrator.

E for England

While racism has been addressed domestically, media attention has focused with far more alacrity on the behaviour of English fans abroad. The xenophobic bigotry of English fans when following the national side has received wide public attention, led by an all too eager tabloid press whose own nationalistic language is overlooked when sifting through the debris of another smashed up bar on the continent. The behaviour of fans abroad is vigilantly captured by both Buford and Ward. When in Germany Buford proclaims how he had forgotten "just how violent the violent nationalism of the English football supporter could be" (1991, p.230) and Ward describes how he sees the English fan on tour:

> You only have to look at the insularity of many English people abroad. They do not travel to see foreign countries and customs; they merely transfer England and their Englishness somewhere else. They travel en masse to destinations where English food and pubs abound; the only difference is the 24-hour drinking (Ward, 1989, p.184).

This passage neatly summarizes how the ideology of nationalism is a dual process which differentiates 'us' from 'strange' foreigners and unites people with the same national identity and values through the reproduction of 'our' way of life, particularly when on foreign soil. The trope of 'Englishness' at Italia '90 was consciously paraded through song and Union Jack shorts topped with a bulldog T-shirt or lobster-coloured suntan. Watching the spectacle of the World Cup 1990 on the terraces and in the streets Dave Hill suggested that the "tournament becomes a kind of allegory for the potential of the human spirit" (*The Independent On Sunday, 24.6.90*). However, after praising the colourful carnivalesque nature of football's 'global village' taking a trip "into the weirder waters of global Post-Modernity", Hill could find no empathy with the England fans. Suggesting that he could not have imagined a more "meek and inadequate spectacle" Hill argued that "lack of worldly wisdom" leads England fans into a mob mentality "reduced by its own neurosis" to assert its "scatological" and "misogynistic" hatred of anything which is alien. He concludes:

> We all know that football thuggery is no longer uniquely English and that English football thugs are no longer uniquely foul. But no other nation produces supporters that are so sourly, so uniformly uncooperative. There is nothing very frightening about most of them. But what utterly depressing company they are (*The Independent On Sunday*, 24.6.90).

The hard bitten attitude of the 'Brits Abroad' - the exchange in national nomenclature from English to British and vice-versa signifies England's imperial cultural formation - has been scrutinized so thoroughly by the press since the 1970s that a journalistic paralysis has emerged: English football fan copy inevitably becomes hooligan copy. Compare the public imagination of English fans abroad with that of the Scottish or Irish and it makes for significantly different reading. For instance, as the 'Tartan Army" rolled into Genoa in Italy, Hill describes the Scots as "affable, sober and preparing for the worst". After the unthinkable (yet predictable) defeat against Costa Rica Hill lamented: In defeat, the Scots made you almost proud to be British.

This bonhomie for Scottish fans is deliberately juxtaposed to the behaviour and morale of their English counterparts. The turnaround of the Scottish fan persona from a violent and drunken expression of machismo to one of a harmless association with alcohol consumption has been declared by Richard Giulianotti (1991) to be an instance of what Foucault identified as 'individuation'. By negatively defining themselves against "an ossified typology of Englishness", Scots fans were able to transcend the surveillance and control of both the authorities and the media through "modes of self-knowledge and empowerment", thus highlighting their "friendly interaction" and "self promotion".

The narrative structures of the media and the law were cranked up once more in readiness for the 1992 European Championships in Sweden. One particularly interesting affront to the 'English Disease' appeared in the glossy *FHM* (*For Him Magazine*) which constructs its articles with the mythological 'new man' in mind. Written in a typically 'hyperreal' form, slotted in between the fashion picks and Hollywood gossip Adrian Porter took a 'personal view of the combatants'. Under the heading 'Export Strength' Porter depicts the English fan abroad as the 'Darling Buds of hell' suggesting:

> England fans by and large are the white trash of the suburbs, mainly from the south of England, who eschew their version of 'patriotism' safe in the knowledge that they are more likely to be deported than convicted, live in dirt for a month, carry colours and pretend they are 'real men'. They are not. Don't forget that 1990 was not only World Cup Hooligan year but also the year of the lager lout. They are one and the same (*FHM*, May 1992).

The unabashed parade of masculinity by England fans abroad is a matter for concern, specifically for victims of aggressive and violent behaviour, which does erupt where large crowds of young men assert their national identity. However, articles like the above, plus other social and legal processes, conspire within a fatal strategy which exacerbates the potential of violent situations before the event itself. For instance, the NFIU, heavily involved in the Swedish police operation as 'advisors', were reported to be using the FBI endorsed 'Photophone', a computer system which identifies 'troublemakers in seconds', heightening the panoply of technological surveillance. Restrictions on North Sea ferries to Sweden compounded problems faced by fans - as it had for Manchester United fans travelling to Rotterdam for the European Cup Winners Cup Final in 1991 - and once in Sweden police made it clear that English fans were unwanted in certain areas of the country by restricting places of accommodation. Such legal and social regulation signifies to the fan that they are entering a potentially hostile environment, where personal liberties are curtailed and a general atmosphere of mistrust prevails. Intense surveillance and restrictive practices - anticipated and planned many months in advance - often ignore attempts by fans themselves to calmly interpose at moments of tension to provide a form of self-regulation. Moreover, the FSA has attempted at both the World Cup in Italy and the European Championships in Sweden to explicitly intervene in the policing of English fans and their media image at home and abroad. The World Cup Campaign, coordinated by Steve Beauchampe, was a visible attempt to enhance the quality of what many people would regard as their annual holiday, and by setting up a Football Embassy, liaising with the Italian authorities, offering advice on accommodation, ticketing, leisure activities and policing problems. Many England fans recognize the importance of making a good impression in Italy, as this article written before the Finals stressed:

> The World Cup is a great opportunity to show everyone that English football fans are brilliant and can be welcomed anywhere. The prize is a return to European Competition for our clubs and not having to listen to the birch 'em brigade spouting off in the press. Failure could mean a ban on the England team and the resurrection of Thatcher's ID card scheme (*Hit The Bar*, Issue 28).

It was attitudes such as these allied to the FSA's initiatives of organizing 5-a-side games with locals, producing 'Friendship Through Football' T-shirts and generally maintaining a high profile which impressed the foreign authorities despite the intimidating circumstances.

In a report of his experiences in Italy (*Football Supporter*, August/September 1990) Beauchampe scathingly attacked the indiscriminate tactics of the police (Caribinieri) who, with preconceived ideas of English supporters - endorsed by our own Minister for Sport, Colin Moynihan, and the NFIU who had predicted a war of the 'super-hooligans' - were responsible for numerous skirmishes and the eventual deportation of 247 England fans from Rimini. This unprecedented deportation of many innocent supporters prompted the FSA to take legal advice on the fans' behalf, lodging Notices of Appeal against the orders through Italian lawyers and petitioning both the European Commission of Human Rights and the European Parliament. In the immediate aftermath of the Rimini disturbances the FSA had collected testimonies of those involved and it became clear that many English fans were horrified and angered by what they had witnessed. By defending the rights of the fans to travel abroad, portraying positive images of fandom, the FSA challenged the hegemonic typology of England fans. The return of English club sides into European competition in 1990/91 strengthened the belief that English football fans could, given the correct circumstances, provide a carnivalesque atmosphere which is peculiarly English yet non-violent. As Manchester United progressed through the Cup Winners Cup competition their supporter's brand of Englishness was born out of the hedonistic youth culture which had taken a hold in the North West in the late 80s/early 90s. The media's fascination with 'Madchester', however much hyped, had documented a noticeable shift in the city's popular culture which had a reciprocal effect on the football terraces. The adopted Monty Python chorus of 'Always Look On The Bright Side Of Life' indicated the prevailing mood of United fans as they successfully made their way across Europe - to Montpellier, Warsaw and finally Rotterdam - in spite of media moral panics about Manchester being a 'Drug economy in recession', ferry companies refusing to take football fans, ticket restrictions imposed by the football club itself, intense police surveillance especially in France and rumours of neo-Nazi groups threatening violence from various corners of Europe. As one of the most criticized, yet popular, fanzines *Red Issue* put it in its celebratory issue of August 1991:

After the trip to Rotterdam at the end of last season, it's hard to believe that anything that happens at Old Trafford this season will be anything more than an anti-climax in comparison to that wet Wednesday in Holland. Grown men crying, enough beer sunk to fill the Irwell, and stories of exploits in the red light district of Amsterdam that would make Mary Whitehouse's hair stand on end. It was the football trip of a lifetime as far as most Red's are concerned, and the team will have to produce greater exploits on the pitch, to give us anything like that night again (*Red Issue, Vol. 4*, No. 1).

Previous trips abroad by England fans, before Heysel and the European ban, had also witnessed high jinx and celebrations which evoke special memories for many supporters of domestic clubs. These memories run counter to the portrayal of English fans' excursions abroad given in the 'hooligan biographies' of Buford and Ward. Richard Brentnall's *Jaunt Account* published in 1990, tells of his exploits while following West Bromwich Albion during their heady days in Europe in the late 70s/early 80s. With humorous anecdotes about trips to Spain, Portugal, Yugoslavia and East Germany, his account captures the full array of emotions football fans experience while following their team on the continent. His nostalgic excavation into "Following the game with high interest and no discredit" is indicative of numerous articles which appear in fanzines that reminisce previous glories in Europe. While some of these anecdotes can be accused of being romantic, rosy re-representations, they frequently offer a far more identifiable form of memoir for the majority of supporters than the 'hooligan biographies'.

It is establishing a common language through talking or writing about football which unifies disparate groups in a celebration of difference with a shared passion for the game. This is true not only nationally but also internationally. It is to the contradictory processes of globalization and nationalism as witnessed within football fandom that we now turn.

The new football order

Football is the universal sport in the world. The celebration of the game often transcends national and political lines of division. The increasing convergence of football styles at both international and club level (i.e. 'Europeanization' of Brazil and the concentration of the world's best players in Italy's Serie A) is allied to the convergence of the mass media and the interests of the economically powerful football nations and clubs. In England, traditionally an isolationist football nation, the transfer of Paul Gascoigne, David Platt and Des Walker to Italian League clubs, has prompted the screening of Serie A football on Channel 4, signifying a broader interest in the European game. Ideas of a European League, partially realized by the league system introduced in the European Cup, corresponds with broader moves among nation states towards European economic union. The collapse of state socialist societies in Eastern Europe led to a euphoric belief that liberal democracy would become the dominant political model throughout the continent, motivated by a notion of European citizenship. However, these myriad universalizing processes have been checked by dissenting voices from various sections of the political spectrum within Western Europe and an aggressive, desperate nationalism, particularly in the 'liberated' Eastern European states. The social anxiety caused by political instability has led to an outbreak of often violent racism and the increasing threat of coherent fascist organizations. Tighter controls on immigration have been called for by right-wing activist groups and individuals in attempts to develop 'cultural purity'. In football, UEFA'S restrictions on overseas players has come into direct conflict with EC regulations on the freedom of movement of EEC nationals within the member states. From 1992 overseas players will be designated by the EC as those from outside the EEC, converse to EUFA's own ruling. The flood of 'football refugees' from the previous country of Yugoslavia is the largest diaspora of footballing talent from a European nation (Duke 1991a). Here, the idea of a civic culture based on tolerance and universal politics became elusive, replaced by immediate passions based on ethnicity, blood and parochial commitments. The cultural warning signs of Yugoslavia's civil war were enacted on the football terraces where the violence reached unprecedented levels, each game played within a volatile atmosphere, the profusion of flares and fireworks creating the aura of a battlefield within stadiums across the country. The process of Perestroika in Eastern Europe has reawoken premodern sources of cultural identity. The re-unification of Germany has raised fears as to the rise of neo-Nazi groups, particularly in the east. Football related violence early in November 1990 at Leipzig, where one supporter was shot, led to the cancellation of a final celebratory match before reunification between East and West Germany due to be played later in the month at the same venue (*The European*, 23.11.90). Followers of the German national team are now gaining similar status - in media and legal discourses - as that of England supporters. With the knowledge of the ostricization England fans face in major tournaments from the carnival atmosphere enjoyed by other European fans - most notably the Danes and the Scots - German fans are in danger of falling foul of a similar self-fulfilling prophecy, their image imploding into the media

143

saturated world of 'hooligan watching'.

Are there any counter-processes within European football to the aggressive, insular and vindictive forms of nationalism described above? In Germany one group of fans have managed to make small but significant inroads into fascist football supporters. Supporters of St. Pauli in Hamburg have managed to integrate a love of football with anti-racist/fascist politics, epitomized by their fanzine *Millerntoar Roar* (named after the ground). Along with the production of a fanzine the fans, under the slogan "never again war, never again fascism, never again Second Division", have produced and distributed stickers, banners, badges, and a video to get their message across. *Millerntoar Roar* gained notoriety as the alternative voice of German football within the UK's rapidly expanding alternative football network. Paying homage to the 'St. Pauli experience' the fanzine *Rodney Rodney* alluded in English terms to this refreshing German football imagination:

> Imagine a club with a catchment area which combines Belfast's Falls Road and Liverpool docks together with London's Soho and Notting Hill. Imagine this ground has no segregation, but anybody making monkey noises at the opposition's black players is intimidated into silence by hundreds of punk anarchists chanting 'Nazi's Out'. Imagine that the keeper takes the field giving the clenched fist salute and goes on demonstrations to support local squatters ... Imagine a new religion for the alienated, the unemployed, the hilarious and the Left (*Rodney Rodney*, No. 5).

The religion is football and the setting could be many major cities in the world. Since the explosion of fanzines in the UK, similar publications have surfaced across Europe. In Germany, a mixture of fan literature has emerged, from fanzines of the UK variety with English names like *Terrace Talk* (Cologne), to fan club newsletters such as *Westkurve* (HSV Hamburg) and 'hooligan zines' like *Molotov* (Duisburg). An extensive list of these magazines is provided in *Das Fanzinebuch* compiled by Dieter Bott in Dusseldorf. Supporters in other countries have also used the UK fanzine format for their own purposes. For example: *Rojo, Blanco y Azul* (covering the three teams of Madrid, Spain); *Stahl Express* (Stahl Linz, Austria); *The Stockholmian* (produced c/o the 'Black Army' of Alk Stockholm, Sweden); and *Ein Staff Og et Sjoimord* and *Apestreken* (both from Norway). The Austrian fanzine *Schwarz auf Weis* (Weiner Sportclub) which means 'black on white' is typical of many European fanzines influenced by the UK fanzine explosion with comic strips, accounts of away trips and erudite articles against mergers and a proposed Super-League. However, it departs from many of the UK publications in its strong ecological and social consciousness - the fanzine, printed on recycled paper, is staunchly opposed to 'right-wing' supporters, donating all its profits to the clubs' youth team and appears to have as many female as male contributors.

The mixing and matching of European youth and popular culture can be explicitly seen within spectator styles. Interest in English football across the continent is frequently born out of the historical roots of the game, but also a fascination with its fans. While the 'English Disease' has become a European phenomenon there are signs that the 'English antidote' is also taking root. English chants are plundered and parodied, particularly by the Italian Ultras who have even been known to wave inflatable bananas as part of their pyrotechnic spectacle of the curva (the home end). An Italian football magazine *Supertifo* (Superfan) offers lavish colour prints of Italian Ultras and occasionally of the traditional English 'kop'. Published monthly it provides an opportunity for fans - of numerous sports - to revel in their own spectacle. Instead of the subversive nature of UK fanzines these glossy magazines, filled with adverts, are *of* the fans rather than by the fans. The extensive newspaper and television coverage of football in countries like Italy has, to a certain degree, lessened the desire or the need for supporters in these countries to produce their own literature as a form of subversive communication. The possibility of watching football from all over Europe is commonplace across the continent, except in the UK where access is only just beginning to develop.

It is the insular nature of the UK's mainstream media that has motivated fans in Britain to produce fanzines which focus on the joys of football in other countries. *Elfmeter* (A British Look At German Football) is the most renowned fanzine of this genre. Originally produced in North Wales, and now from Staffordshire, *Elfmeter* (meaning 'penalty kick') carries all sorts of minutiae from the bundesliga and was at the forefront of British continental football fanzine publication. Other explorations in this field offer a hybrid of statistical information and match details with a form of football travel writing. Most notably *A Traveller's Guide To Greek Football*

'91 with details of forty clubs, ground directions, photographs and travel information. Even more obscure is *Albania FC* by Dave Twydell, billed as "A lighthearted but factual account of football in Albania" written in 1989. Many of these investigative accounts of football on the continent strive to celebrate rather than erase difference, providing an alternative to staid approaches to a common European popular culture, symbolized by the Eurovision Song contest, which is increasingly stagnant in terms of its creativity.

Amongst UK fanzines, particularly those on football in general, an interest in the global welfare of the sport has grown appreciably as editors strive for more novel and investigative football stories. *WSC*'s exploration of African and South American football echoes the broader globalization of nation cultures. Whether it is priming its readers on the finer points of Egyptian football before the 1990 World Cup (*WSC*, No. 35) or a review of the 1991 'Copa America' in Chile (*WSC*, No. 55) the magazine has sought to broaden the football knowledge of its audience. While domestic issues and anecdotes still take precedent, the magazine has pioneered a fascination with the world game, revelling in the difference and nuances of football from other continents. The globalization of different football cultures and its subsequent celebration parallels the re-discovery or re-invention of 'world music' "a kind of folk revival for the late-twentieth century" (Redhead, 1990, p.53) which is grounded in folk ideology. While it is dangerous to pursue the allegorical treatment of world football with world music too far, it is significant that one of the early protagonists of the merits of both football fanzines and African music (most notably The Bhundu Boys) is DJ John Peel. Peel's radio programmes, particularly in the mid to late 80s, signified a specific taste culture, derived from a 'punk ethic' and style, which embraced an internationalist view of popular culture, grounded in the language of community, authenticity and origins.

Football fanzines form part of a new affective sensibility and relationship to the world (Grossberg, 1987, p.186), capturing new moods, feelings, and desires through varying degrees of concern and energy for the future of the sport, in both parochial and global senses. Football fanzines are also part of a 'culture of defence' which has developed in opposition to specific modernizing processes within the game (enforced all-seater stadiums, increased commercialization, heightened influence of television companies and sponsors) and specific social and legal regulations (the shelved ID Card scheme and the intense media focus and re-representation of football fans). This work has attempted to critically document the rise of fanzines as an integral part of the new affective sensibility within football - from its subcultural roots in punk to its bricolage of football nostalgia and satirical humour - analysing textual content and tracing the ontology of the 'alternative football fan network'. The unprecedented growth of the subculture suggests that football fanzines are here to stay, and may only be superseded by the potentially more subversive medium of portable video. Football fanzines' sustainability is in contrast to that of popular music fanzines mainly because supporters invariably follow a club for life and there is always a new generation of eager young fans to take their mantle. There are, quite reasonably, fears that many children that follow football choose to support the bigger and more successful clubs (Manchester United, Liverpool, Arsenal), however, fanzines appear to be one form of defence against such domination, every League club and the majority of non-league clubs have a fanzine dedicated to the success of their team.

10   Fifteen fame filled minutes of the fanzine writer

Fanzines have become a firmly established part of football subculture. Across the grounds of Britain the sight of supporters thumbing through the latest issue of one of their club's fanzines is as commonplace as that of fans perusing the back page of the match programme to check the team-sheet. Similarly, the reading and collecting of fanzines mirrors an older tradition of collecting programmes, a pastime enthusiastically documented by Phil Shaw (1980). The sheer volume of football fanzines produced since the mid 1980s represents an unprecedented form of cultural consumption actively turned into cultural production.

With myriad titles, ingenious layouts, individualized use of typography, and richly imaginative ways of writing about football (in many instances parodying traditional forms of football journalism by recourse to disparate everyday experiences ironically pieced together) football fanzines, as a popular cultural form, have an analogy with the idea of *bricolage* as developed by subcultural theorists at Birmingham's Centre for Contemporary Cultural Studies. The football fanzine editor is the contemporary cultural bricoleur, an 'odd-job man' in the production of cultural meaning, and creating an aesthetic which relies on computer literacy and desk-top publishing skills, where previously the DIY of punk fanzines relied on the technique of 'cut 'n' paste' and the availability of a photocopier (see Chapter 3). A hybrid of football related experiences (going to matches; listening to radio commentaries; watching televised games; reading match reports or football magazines; collecting football ephemera, such as posters or stickers; playing simulated football board and action games, like 'Subbuteo'; and, perhaps most importantly, playing the game itself) and other popular discourses (both social and ideological) have been infused, resulting in a new and distinctive 'football imagination' - a new style of football writing and expression. Football fanzines have emerged as a rare oppositional style to the highly commercialized, yet overtly insular and corrupt, football industry. As documented in Chapter 4, football fanzine subculture emerged out of obsession and enthusiasm for the sport, allied with anger induced by inept administration within the game, the panoptical gaze of the police and the Thatcher government, and the heightened sense of moral panic by the tabloid press. A newly found desire to defend the name of football supporters in opposition to their re-representation by the media led to the direct intervention, through the production of fanzines, into the media industry itself, most notably with the success of the fan magazine *When Saturday Comes* (see Haynes, 1993). A cultural commitment to change in the way the game is controlled and managed, in terms of the supporters relationships with the clubs, the football authorities, the police, the media, the Government, and other fan groups, led to affective alliances among supporters. Fanzines supplied an 'alternative football fan network' to enable the sharing of desires, fears and ideas about the modern game.

As documented in Chapters 2 and 3, football fanzines have genealogical roots in the alternative press and the satirical movement in the sixties and early seventies, which spawned within the realm of football, the alternative magazine *Foul*. It was *Foul*'s humour which helped negate the effects of what Ian Taylor (1971) theorized as the 'bourgeoisification' and 'internationalization' of the game, which fractured the perceived 'participatory democracy' that fans had with the club they supported up to the late 1950s and early 1960s. However, nearly a decade after *Foul*'s demise, in the aftermath of the disasters at Bradford and Heysel in 1985, it seemed no laughing matter to be a football fan in England. Victimized by policing, vilified by the press, English fans found that their clubs were ostracized from European competition, and that their position on the terraces was literally crumbling under their feet as money was ploughed into building executive boxes at the expense of wider improvements of facilities for the general punter. The executive box, designed for corporate entertainment, was the football industry's form of gentrification, a symbol of Thatcherite 'enterprise culture', and as in wider society, something only a minority could capitalize on.

Meanwhile, the tragic events of 1985 ensured that the majority of fans were subordinate to the increased surveillance at football matches, both within and without the ground, as a result of the legislation augmented by the Thatcher government (Chapter 5). As I argued in Chapter 3, the re-invigorated authoritarianism of the Thatcher government, built on multiple discourses of 'law and order', saw the most intensive efforts to subordinate football related violence. By the mid eighties the 'football hooligan' had become the bogeyman of English society.

The burlesque 'scallydom' of the Liverpool fanzine *The End* offered one avenue of conscious resistance to the prevailing ideology of the Tory Government towards the football industry and 'youth culture' in general. The fanzine puts into focus the contradictory nature of youth culture's relationship with the football industry as the sartorial style of the 'football casual' challenged and broadened what was deemed 'suitable' for men to wear at the match, while continuing to assimilate regional rivalries which had been accentuated by the economic and social policies of the Government.

Yet *The End* despite its originality was a solitary profane voice from the terraces, until what can be considered to be the political watershed of 1985, with regard to fans' active participation in the politics of the game. While the Popplewell Inquiry of 1986 sought to further the implementation of repressive legislation at football grounds, an equally stubborn defence of the football consumer, the fan, was also gaining ground. The fresh irreverence and investigative cynicism of *Off The Ball*, *When Saturday Comes*, and *The Absolute Game* encouraged, through their listing and promotion of new football fanzines, a creative spirit which exposed and cast into doubt the workings of the football industry and related issues of policing and media influence. Having interviewed and corresponded with many of those involved in the writing, editing and distribution of fanzines in the formative years of the phenomenon it is clear that many were surprised by, and never foresaw, the shared sense of outrage which their humbly compiled anecdotes and cartoons enjoyed with their fellow supporters. The existence of some form of networking between fanzine editors, their readers and independent supporters organizations, most notably the FSA, implies a coherent cultural politics based upon several key issues: the modernization of football stadia; the governance of the football industry, including policing; mass media re-representations of football fans; and finally, the relationship between supporters and the club they support (or oppose). This popular cultural formation suggests a dialectic between individual and collective agency, where an individual's love of the game emerges from the desire for communication among fellow supporters. The team game of football and its support emphasizes the fact that the sport is eminently social, yet complex. The mushrooming of football fanzines gave a fillip to the political agency of supporters, enabling alliances and creative possibilities to undermine stereotypical discourses of football fans in attempting to gain credibility in wider public domains.

The wider political domain also began to filter into the new football consciousness. *Born Kicking* (women's football), *Marching Altogether* Leeds Fan's United Against Racism and Fascism), and *The Football Pink* (Gay Supporters Association) all represent fanzines with strong cultural and political messages designed to transgress the dominant discourses of sexism, racism and homophobia. The football stadium remains a heavily masculinized arena, but football fanzines do open up the possibility for alternative narratives on the construction of gender and sexuality within the sport (Haynes, 1993a).

To conclude, fanzines are a novel, irreverent gaze upon the world of football contributing to a wider oral tradition of talking about the game either at the match, the pub or the workplace. The affective alliances between fans and the game belies the manner in which they are frequently mistreated by the football authorities, the clubs and the police. As the media saturation of the FA Premier League and the European Champions League increasingly attracts the groundswell of new, younger supporters the following for smaller clubs will continue to dwindle. Football fanzines offer one form of defence to the erosion of a varied and vibrant football culture by sustaining interest in all professional and semi-professional clubs in the UK.

Fanzine bibliography

The Abbey Rabbit (Cambridge United)
The Absolute Game (Scotland)
And Smith Must Score (Brighton and Hove Albion)
Apestreken (Norway)
Are You Sitting Comfortably? (South East)
Attack (Norwich City)

Beyond the Boundary (Oldham Athletic)
Blow Football (Subbuteo)
Blueprint (Manchester City)
Born Kicking (Women's Football)
Boy's Own (Music/Football)

C-Stander (Derby County)
City Gent (Bradford City)
Come on Dagenham Use Your Forwards (Dagenham)
D-Pleated (Luton Town)
Dial M for Mrthyr (Mrthyr Tydfil)

Ein Staff Og et Sjoimord (Norway)
Elfmeter (British/German)
The End (Music/Football)
Every Man A Football Artist (Kilkenny City)

Fly Me to the Moon (Middlesbrough Town)
Flashing Blade (Sheffield United)
Football Supporter (FSA)

Fortunes Always Hiding (West Ham United)
Foul (70s/General)
From the Grove to the Harrow (Berwick Rangers)

Get Lawrence On (Basingstoke)
The Gibbering Clairvoyant (Dumbarton)
The Gooner (Arsenal)
Grorty Dick (West Bromwich Albion)
Gulls Eye (Brighton and Hove Albion)

The Hanging Sheep (Leeds United)
Hit the Bar (General)

Imperfect Match (Arsenal)
In the Loft (Queens Park Rangers)

King of the Kippax (Manchester City)

The Lad Done Brilliant (Humour)
The Lion's Roar (Milwall)
Liverpool Are on the Telly Again (Norwich City)
A Load of Bull (Wolves)
A Love Supreme (Sunderland)

The Magic Sponge (Leeds United)
Marching Together (Leeds United)
Mi Whippets Dead (Rotherham United)
Millerntoar Roar (St. Pauli)
Mission Impossible (Darlington)
Mission Terminated (Torquay United)
Molotov (Duisburg)
Monkey Business (Hartlepool United)
My Eyes Have Seen the Glory (Tottenham Hotspur)

A Nightmare on Dee Street (Glentoran)
No Idle Talk (Hearts)
No One Likes Us (Milwall)
A Novel School of Thought (London)

The Occasional Terrorist (Tooting and Mitcham)
Off The Ball (General)
The One and Only (General)
On The March (Southampton)
Orienteer (Leyton Orient)
Our Day Will Come (Manchester United/Celtic)
The Pie (Notts County)
Pretty in Pink (Brighton and Hove Albion)
The Proclaimer (Hibernian)
Psycho Arab (Dundee United)

Rebels Without A Clue (Slough Town)
Reclaim the Game (FSA)
Red Issue (Manchester United)
Reliant Robin (Wrexham)
Rodney, Rodney (General)
Rojo, Blanco y Azul (Madrid, Spain)

Schwartz auf Weis (Weiner Sportclub)
Scottish Zine Scene (Scottish)
The Shankhill Skinhead (Manchester United)
Sing When We're Fishing (Grimsby Town)
Sing When We're Ploughin' (Norwich City
Someone Likes Us (Milwall)
The Spur (Tottenham Hotspur)
The Square Ball (Leeds United)
Stahl Express (Stahl Linz)
The Stockholmian (Alk Stockholm)
Supertifo (Italy)

Tackler (General)
Talk of the Toon (Newcastle United)
Terrace Talk (Cologne)
Terrace Talk (York City)
There's Only One F in Fulham (Fulham)
Tomato Soup and Lentils (Leeds United/Arbroath)
A Traveller's Guide to Greek Football '91 (British/Greek)

United We Stand (Manchester United)

Voice of the Valley (Charlton Athletic)

Waiting for the Great Leap Forward (Motherwell)
Walking Down the Halbeath Road (Dumfermiline Athletic)
We Hate Jimmy Hill (General Scottish)
Westkurve (HSV Hamburg)
What's the Score? (Liverpool)
When Saturday Comes (General)
When Sunday Comes (General)
Wise Men Say (Sunderland)
World Shut Your Mouth (Rangers)

Many of the fanzines listed above no longer exist, many have changed name, and may have new editors and writers. This is the nature of football fanzine culture. However, a more extensive list is continually updated within *When Saturday Comes*. For more information on defunct fanzines there is an extensive archive of fanzines past and present within the Manchester *Institute* for Popular Culture, at The Manchester Metropolitan University.

Bibliography

Adorno, T., 1991, *The Culture Industry*, Routledge, London.

Archetti, E.P., 1992, 'Argentinian Football: A Ritual of Violence?', *The International Journal of the History of Sport*. Vol.9, No.2.

Armstrong, G., 1992, '...Like that Desmond Morris?'. Unpublished paper, Department of Anthropology, University of London.

Allan, J., 1989, *Bloody Casuals: Diary of a Football Hooligan*. Famedram, Northern.

Allen, R., 1970, *Skinhead*. New English Library, London.

Bale, J., 1991, 'Playing at home: British football and a sense of place', in J. Williams and S. Wagg (eds.), *British Football and Social Change: Getting Into Europe*, Leicester University Press, Leicester.

Baudrillard, J., 1987, *The Evil Demon of Images*, Power Institute of Fine Arts, Sydney.

Bishop, J. and Hoggart, P., 1986, *Organising Around Enthusiasms: Mutual Aid in Leisure*, Comedia, London.

Bromberger, C., 1993, 'Fireworks and the Ass', in S. Redhead (ed.), *The Passion and the Fashion: Football Fandom in the New Europe*. Avebury, Aldershot.

Bromberger, C., Hayot, A. and Mariottini, J. M., 1993, 'Allez L'OM, Forza Juve: The Passion for Football in Marseille and Turin' in S. Redhead (ed.), *The Passion and the Fashion: Football Fandom in the New Europe,*Avebury, Aldershot.

Buford, B., 1991, *Among The Thugs*, Secker and Warburg, London.

Burton, F. and Carlen, P., 1979, *Official Discourse*, Routledge and Kegan Paul, London.

Cahn, S. K., 1993, 'From the "Muscle Moll" to the "Butch" Ballplayer: Mannishness, Lesbianism, and Homophobia in US Women's Sport" in *Feminist Studies,* Vol. 19 (2), pp.342-364

Chambers, I., 1985, *Urban Rhythms: Pop Music and Popular Culture*, Macmillan, London.

Chambers, I., 1990, *Border Dialogues: Journeys in Postmodernity*, Routledge, London.

Clarke, A., 1991, 'Figuring A Brighter Future', in E. Dunning and C. Rojek (eds.), *Sport and Leisure in the Civilising Process*, Macmillan, London.

Cockburn, C., 1988, 'Masculinity, the Left and feminism', in R. Chapman and J. Rutherford (eds), *Male Order: Unwrapping Masculinity*, Lawrence and Wishart, London.

Cohen, S., 1971, *Images of Deviance*, Penguin, Harmondsworth.

Collier, S., 1991, 'Repositioning the New Man: Sex, Work and the New Men's Magazines'. Occasional Paper, Department of Law, University of Newcastle upon Tyne.

Cosgrove, S., 1991, *Hampdon Babylon*, Canongate, Edinburgh.

Curren, M., and Redmond, L., 1991, 'We'll Support You Evermore? Football Club Allegience - A Survey of When Saturday Comes Readers'. IT Working Paper, Sir Norman Chester Centre for Football Research, University of Leicester.

Davies, H., 1972, *The Glory Game: A Year In The Life Of Tottenham Hotspur*, Mainstream, Edinburgh.

Davies, P., 1990, *All Played Out*, Heineman, London.

Dougan, D., 1970, 'Football is a man's game', in W. Luscombe (ed.), *The Park Drive Book of Football*, Pelham Books, London.

Duke, V., 1991, 'The sociology of football: a research agenda for the 1990s', *The Sociological Review*, Vol.39, No.3.

Duke, V., 1991a, 'The flood from the East? Perestroika and the migration of footballers from Eastern Europe'. Paper presented at the International Migration of Sports Talent Conference, University of Keele, 1991.

Duke, V., 1991b, 'The politics of football in the new Europe' in J. Williams and S. Wagg (eds.), *British Football and Social Change: Getting Into Europe*, Leicester University Press, Leicester.

Dunning, E., 1989, 'The Figurational Approach to Leisure and Sport', in C. Rojek (ed.), *Leisure for Leisure*, Macmillan, London.

Dunning, E., 1992, 'The Social Roots of Football Hooliganism Violence: a Reply to the Critics of the Leicester School'. Paper presented at the International Conference, Soccer: Culture and Identity, University of Aberdeen, 1992.

Dunning, E., Murphy, P. and Williams, J., 1988, *The Roots of Football Hooliganism: A Sociological and Historical Study*, Routledge and Kegan Paul, London.

Dunning, E., Murphy, P. and Waddington, I., 1991, 'Anthropoligical Versus Sociological Approaches to the Study of Football Hooliganism: Some Critical Notes', *The Sociological Review*, Vol.39, No.3.

Dunphy, E., 1976, *Only A Game: The Diary of a Professional Footballer* Penguin, London.

Dunphy, E., 1991, *A Strange Kind of Glory: Sir Matt Busby and Manchester United*, Heineman, London.

Eco, U., 1986, *Travels In Hyperreality*, Picador, London.

Featherstone, M,. 1991, *Consumer Culture and Postmodrnism*, Sage, London.

Fishwick, N., 1989, *English Football and Society, 1910 - 1950*. Manchester University Press, Manchester.

Fiske, J., 1989, *Understanding Popular Culture*, Unwin Hynman, London.

Football Association, 1991, *Blueprint for the Future of Football*. London.

Foucault, M., 1991, *Foucault Effect*, MacMillan, London.

Foucault, M., 1991, 'Politics and the study of discourse' in G. Burchell, C. Gordon, and P. Miller (eds.), *The Foucault Effect: Studies in Governmentality*, Harvester Wheatsheaf, Hemel Hempstead.

Fynn, A. and Guest, L., 1991, *Heroes and Villains*, Penguin, London.

Gamble, A., 1988, *The Free Economy and the Strong State: The Politics of Thatcherism*, Macmillan, London.

Gane, M., 1991, *Baudrillard: Critical and Fatal Theory*, Routledge, London.

Gane, M., 1991, *Baudrillard's Bestiary: Baudrillard and Culture*, Routledge, London.

Geraghty, P., Simpson and Whannel, G. 1986, 'Tunnel Vision: Television's World Cup', in A. Tomlinson and G. Whannel (eds.), *Off The Ball: The Football World Cup*, Pluto, London.

Giulianotti, R., 1991, 'The Tartan Army in Italy: the case for the carnivalesque', *The Sociological Review*. Vol.39, No.3.

Giulianotti, R., 1991a, 'Keep it in the Family: an Outline of Hibs Casuals' Social Ontology'. Department of Sociology, University of Aberdeen

Giulianotti, R., 1992, 'Soccer Casuals as cultural Intermediaries: The Cultural Politics of Scottish Style'. Department of Sociology, University of Aberdeen.

Green, G., 1974, *Soccer In The Fifties*, Ian Allan, London.

Grossberg, L., 1987, 'Rock and Roll in Search of an Audience', in J. Lull (ed.), *Popular Music and Communication*, Sage, London.

Grossberg, L., 1992, 'Is There a fan in the house?: The Affective Sensibility of Fandom', in C. A. Lewis (ed.), *The Adoring Audience*, Routledge, London.

Hall, S., 1978, 'The Treatment of football hooliganism in the Press', in R. Ingham (ed.), *Football Hooliganism: The Wider Context*, Inter Action Print, London.

Hall, S., 1988, *Hard Road To Renewal: Thatcherism and the Crisis of the Left*, Verso, London.

Hall, S. and Jacques, M., (eds.), 1983, *The Politics of Thatcherism*. Lawrence and Wishart, London.

Hall, W. and Parkinson, M., 1973, *Football Report: An Anthology of Soccer*, Sportmans Book Club, Newton Abbot.

Hamilton, I. (ed.), 1992, *The Faber Book of Soccer*, Faber and Faber, London.

Harding, J., 1991, *For The Good Of The Game*, Robson Books.

Hargreaves, John, 1986, *Sport, Power and Culture*. Cambridge: Polity Press.

Hargreaves, J. 1990. 'Gender on the sports agenda', *International Review for the Sociology of Sport*, No. 25.

Harris, M., 1982, 'Leeds, the lads and the meeja', *New Society*. 25.11.82.

Hearn, J., 1992, *Men In The Public Eye: The construction and deconstruction of public men and public patriarchies*, Routledge, London.

Hebdige, D., 1986, *Hiding In The Light: On Images and Things*, Comedia, London.

Hey, V., 1986, *Patriarchy and Pub Culture*, Tavistock, London.

Hill, D., 1989, *Out Of His Skin: The John Barnes Phenomenon*, Faber and Faber, London.

Hoggart, R., 1957, *Uses of Literacy*, Penguin, Harmondsworth.

Hopcraft, A., 1968, *The Football Man: People and Passions in Soccer*, Simon and Schuster, London.

Hornby, N., 1992, *Fever Pitch*, Gollancz, London.

Hornby, N., (ed.), 1993, *My Favourite Year*, H. F. & G. Witherby, London.

Hutchinson, J., 1982, *The Football Industry: The early Years of the Professional Game*, Richard Drew, Glasgow.

James, D. E., 1988, 'Poetry/Punk/Production: Some Recent Writing in L.A.', in E. A. Kaplan (ed.), *Postmodernism and Its Discontents*, Verso, London.

Kuhn, A., 1984, 'Women's Genres', in *Screen*.

Kuhn, A., 1992, *Women's Pictures: Feminism and Cinema*, Verso, London.

Lacey, M., 1989, *El Tel Was A Space Alien Vol. 1*, Juma, Sheffield.

Lacey, M., 1990, *Where's The Bar: A Guide To Non-League Football*. Juma, Sheffield.

Lansdown, H. and Spillius, A., (eds.), 1990, *Saturday's Boys: The Football Experience*, Collins Willow, London.

Layland, J. 1990, 'On the conflicts of doing feminist research into masculinity', in L. Stanley (ed.), *Feminist Praxis: Research Theory and Epistemology in Feminist Sociology*, Routledge, London.

Ledbrooke, A. and Turner, E., 1955, *Soccer From The Press Box*. The Sportsman's Book Club, London.

McRobbie, A. 1991, *Feminism and Youth Culture: From Jackie to Just Seventeen*, Macmillan, London.

McRobbie, A., 1982, 'Jackie: An Ideology of Adolescent Femininity', in B. Waites, T. Bennett and G. Martin (eds.) *Popular Culture: Past and Present*, Croom Helm, London.

Mason, T., 1980, *Association Football and English Society, 1863 - 1915*, Harvester, London.

Mason, T., 1988, *Sport In Britain*, Faber and Faber, London.

Meisl, W., 1956, *Soccer Revolution*, The Sportsman's Book Club, London.

Mercer, K. and Julien, I., 1988, 'Race, Sexual Politics and Black Masculinity: A dossier', in R. Chapman and J. Rutherford (eds.), *Male Order: Unwrapping Masculinity*, Lawrence and Wishart, London.

Metcalf, A., 1986, 'Gay Machismo', in A. Metcalf and M. Humphries (eds), *The Sexuality of Men*, Pluto, London.

Moore, B., 1970, *England! England!* The Sportsman's Book Club, London.

Moorhouse, H. F., 1984, 'Organising Enthusiasm: Specialist Magazines and Sub-Cultures' *Leisure Studies Association Conference Papers*, No.26.

Moorhouse, H. F., 1991, 'On the periphery: Scotland, Scottish football and the new Europe', in J. Williams and W. Wagg (eds.), *British Football and Social Change: Getting into Europe*, Leicester University Press, Leicester.

Mort, F., 1988, 'Boys Own? Masculinity, Styles and Popular Culture', in R. Chapman and J. Rutherford (eds.), *Male Order: Unwrapping Masculinity*, Lawrence and Wishart, London.

Murphy, P., Williams, J. and Dunning, E., 1990, *Football On Trial: Spectator Violence and Development in the Football World*, Routledge, London.

Murray, B., 1984, *The Old Firm: Sectarianism and Society in Scotland*, John Donald, Edinburgh.

Nickolds, A. and Hey, S., 1976, *The Foul Book of Football No.1*.

O'Connor, B. and Boyle, R., 1993, 'Dallas With Balls: televised sport, soap opera and male and female pleasures', *Leisure Studies*, Vol. 12, pp.107-119.

Parkinson, M., 1971, *Football Daft*, Stanley Paul, London.

Pick, J. B., 1958, *The Spectators Handbook*, The Sportsman's Book Club, London.

Pleasance, H., 1991, 'Open or closed: popular magazines and dominant culture', in S. Franklin, C. Lurie and J. Stacey, (eds.), *Off Centre: Feminism and Cultural Studies*, Harper Collins, London.

Popplewell, Mr. Justice, 1986, *Committee of Inquiry into Crowd Safety and Control at Sports Grounds, Final Report*, HMSO, London.

Poster, M., 1990, *Mode of Information: Poststructuralism and*

Social Context, Polity Press, Cambridge.

Redhead, S., 1987, *Sing When You're Winning: The Last Football Book*, Pluto, London.

Redhead, S., 1987a, 'When Men Were Men: Football in Class Struggle', *New Socialist*, No.47.

Redhead, S., 1990, *The End of Century Party: Youth and Pop Towards 2000*, Manchester University Press, Manchester.

Redhead, S., 1990a, 'The Gory Game: Law and the Governance of Football', *European University Institute, Florence, Colloquium Paper, 90.*

Redhead, S., 1991, *Football With Attitude*, Wordsmith, Manchester.

Redhead, S., 1991a, 'The era of the end or the end of an era: Football and youth culture in Britain', in J.Williams and S.Wagg (eds.), *British football and Social Change: Getting into Europe*, Leicester University Press, Leicester.

Redhead, S., 1991b, 'Some reflections on discourses on football hooliganism', *The Sociological Review*, Vol.39, No.3.

Revie, D., 1968, 'Is Modern Football Too Rough?', in G. Banks (ed.) *The Park Drive Book of Football.*, Wolf, Manchester.

Robins, D., 1984, *We Hate Humans*, Penguin, Harmondsworth.

Robins, K. and Cornford, J., 1991, 'Looking Local', *Marxism Today*, November 1991.

Robinson, J., 1989, *The Best of Football Fanzines*, Fanzines Publishing Co.

Rose, A. and Friedman, J., 1992, 'Sports in America: Television Sports As Mas(s)culine Cult of Distraction'. Paper given at Screen Studies Conference, University of Glasgow.

Rowe, D., 1991, '"That Misery of Stringer's Cliches": Sports Writing' *Cultural Studies*, Vol.5, No.1.

Rowe, D., 1992, 'Modes of Sports Writing' in P. Dahlgren and C. Sparks, (eds.), *Journalism and Popular Culture*, Sage, London.

Savage, J., 1991, *England's Dreaming*, Faber and Faber, London.

Seabrook, J., 1978, *What Went Wrong? Working People and the Ideals of the Labour Movement*, Victor Gollanz.

Seabrook, J., 1988, *The Leisure Society*, Basil Blackwell, Oxford.

Shaw, P., 1989, *Whose Game Is It Anyway?* Argus, London.

Shaw, P., 1980, *Collecting Football Programmes*, Granada, London.

Shilling, C., 1991, 'Educating the Body: Physical Capital and the Production of Social Inequalities', *Sociology*, Vol. 25, No. 4.

Taylor, I,. 1971, 'Soccer consciousness and soccer hooliganism', in S. Cohen (ed.), *Images of Deviance*, Penguin, London.

Taylor, I., 1987, 'Putting the boot into a working-class sport: British soccer after Bradford and Brussels' *Sociology of Sport Journal*. 1987.

Taylor, I., 1989, 'Hillsborough, 15 April 1989: Some Personal Contemplations', *New Left Review*, No. 177.

Taylor, I., 1990, 'English Soccer In 1990: Possibilities and Problems', *European University Institute, Florence, Colloqium Paper 123/ 90*.

Taylor, I. 1991. 'English football in the 1990s: taking Hillsborough seriously?', in J. Williams and S. Wagg (eds.), *British Football and Social Change: Getting into Europe*, Leicester University Press, Leicester.

Taylor, Lord Justice, 1990, *The Hillsborough Stadium Disaster (15 April 1989), Final Report*, HMSO, London.

Taylor, R., 1990, 'Puskas and the real thing', in H. Lansdown and A. Spillius (eds.), *Saturdays Boys: The Football Experience*, Collins Willow, London.

Taylor, R., 1991, 'Walking alone together: football supporters and their relationship with the game', in J. Williams and S. Wagg (eds.), *British Football and Social Change: Getting into Europe*, Leicester University Press, Leicester.

Taylor, R. 1992. *Football And Its Fans: Supporters And Their Relationship With The Game, 1885 - 1985*. Leicester: Leicester University Press.

Tischler, M., 1981, *Footballers and Businessmen: The Origins of Professional Soccer in England*, Holmes and Meier, New York.

Tomlinson, A., 1991, 'North and South: the rivalry of the Football League and the Football Association', in J. Williams and S. Wagg (eds.), *British Football and Social Change: Getting into Europe*, Leicester University Press, Leicester.

Tomlinson, A. and Whannel, G.. (eds.), 1986, *Off The Ball: The Football World Cup*, Pluto, London.

Tummon, J., 1991, 'Draft Proposal for Re-Structuring of the Football League', Manchester Football Supporters Association.

Turner, R., 1990, *In Your Blood: Football Culture In The Late 1980s and Early 1990s*, Working Press, London.

Wagg, S. 1984. *The Football World: A Contemporary Social History*. Brighton: Harvester.

Wagg, S., 1991, 'Playing the part: the media and the England Football team', in J. Williams and S. Wagg (eds.), *British Football and Social Change: Getting into Europe*, Leicester University Press, Leicester. '

Wagg, S. and Goldberg, A., 1991, 'It's not a knockout: English football and globalisation', in J. Williams and S. Wagg (eds.), *British Football*

167

and Social Change: Getting into Europe, Leicester University Press, Leicester.

Wakefield, N., 1990, *Postmodernism: The Twighlight of the Real*, Pluto, London.

Walvin, J., 1975, *The Peoples Game*, Allen Lane, London.

Walvin, J., 1986, *Football and the Decline of Britain*, Macmillan, Basingstoke.

Ward, A. and Alister, I., 1981, *Barnsley: A Study in Football 1953 - 1959*, Crowberry, Staffordshire.

Ward, C., 1989, *Steaming In: Journal of a Football Fan*, Simon and Schuster, London.

Whannel, G., 1979, 'Football Crowd Behaviour and the Press', *Media Culture and Society*.

Whannel, G., 1983, *Blowing the Whistle: The Politics of Sport*, Pluto, London.

Williams, J., Dunning, E. and Murphy, P., 1984, *Hooligans Abroad*, Routledge and Kegan Paul, London. (Reprint 1989).

Williams, J., 1991, 'Having an away day: English football spectators and the hooligan debate', in J. Williams and S. Wagg (eds.), *British Football and Social Change: Getting into Europe*, Leicester University Press, Leicester.

Williams, R., 1961, *The Long Revolution*, Penguin, Harmondsworth.

Winship, J., 1987, *Inside Women's Magazines*, Pandora, London.

Winship, J., 1991, 'The Impossibility of Best: Enterprise meets domesticity in the practical women's magazines of the 1980s', *Cultural Studies*. Vol.5, No.1.

Woodhouse, J., 1991, *A National Survey of Female Football Fans*, Sir

Norman Chester Centre for Football Research, University of Leicester.

Young, K., 1991, 'Sport and Collective Violence', *International Journal of Physical Education*.

RAVE OFF

POLITICS AND DEVIANCE IN CONTEMPORARY YOUTH CULTURE

Edited by STEVE REDHEAD

POPULAR CULTURAL STUDIES: 1

"...recommended as student reading." Youth and Policy

"...stimulating and provocative opening contribution to the Popular Cultural Studies series. Courses on youth culture will look a little incomplete if they do not now include them as set reading ...central texts for any up-to-date specialist course." Leisure Studies Association Newsletter

Steve Redhead and a team of authors associated with the Manchester Institute for Popular Culture at Manchester Metropolitan University have written a unique account of deviant youth culture at the end of the century, concentrating on the much-hyped 'rave' scene and its connections to recreational drug use - for instance Ecstasy - contemporary pop and dance music, youth tourism, football hooliganism and the 'enterprise culture'.

The book attempts to provide answers to such questions as: What is 'rave culture'? What had 'Madchester' got to do with it? Has the rave (formerly acid house) scene merely parodied an earlier moment in pop history (60s psychedelia, 70s punk or Northern Soul)? Is illegal 'party drug' use a passing fad or here to stay? What political and legal implications are there of this new 'hedonism in hard times'? Has 90s youth culture embraced or rejected the values of the market, individualism and enterprise?

1993   208 pages   Hbk   1 85628 463 8   £29.50
Pbk   1 85628 465 4   £12.95

Price subject to change without notification

arena

THE PASSION AND THE FASHION

FOOTBALL FANDOM IN THE NEW EUROPE

Edited by **STEVE REDHEAD**

POPULAR CULTURAL STUDIES: 2

"...intriguing... Christian Bromberger's dissection of Napoli is riveting." The Independent

The culture of the soccer terrace is changing.

The football crowd – and moreover football fandom in general – is undergoing significant change which reflect wider shifts in gender, popular culture, modernity and postmodernity.

Steve Redhead and his colleagues portray this cultural change on the European soccer terrace in a readable book which will be of interest to the general reader and to the specialist in cultural studies, sociology of sport, leisure studies and popular culture. The research reported here draws on specific new studies of the fans of the best known European clubs such as Juventus, Napoli, Leeds United, Marseilles and Manchester United. Some of this research was submitted, on request, to the Home Affairs Committee of the House of Commons and has attracted wide media interest.

| 1993 | 224 pages | Hbk | 1 85628 462 X | £29.95 |
| | Pbk | 1 85628 464 6 | £12.95 | |

Price subject to change without notification

THE LADS IN ACTION

SOCIAL PROCESS IN AN URBAN YOUTH SUBCULTURE

DAVID MOORE

POPULAR CULTURAL STUDIES: 3

"This is a much needed, adventurous work..." Professor David Parkin, University of London

The Lads in Action, based on long-term participant observation with Australian skinheads, portrays the social processes which underlie and constitute the skinhead subculture.

The book begins with a critique of existing studies of youth. Moore then presents a phenomenological analysis of the meaning of skinhead expressive activity for the skinheads themselves, heavily influenced by anthropology of social process. After dispensing with the static concept of 'gang' in favour of a more processural framework, he deals in turn with the meaning of visual and performative style for skinheads, interaction between skinheads and the members of other youth subcultures, the significance of drinking, and the public and private representations skinheads make about the young women with whom they form relationships. He also outlines the part played by 'memories', the stories of past exploits which skinheads tell to one another, in the creation of the skinhead's categorical and personal identity. These issues are examined in the light of extensive ethnographic material.

David Moore is a Visiting Research Fellow in the Addiction Studies Unit, School of Psychology, Curtin University of Technology, Perth.

1994   192 pages   Hbk   1 85742 203 1   £29.50
Pbk   1 85742 204 X   £12.95

Price subject to change without notification

HOSTS AND CHAMPIONS

SOCCER CULTURES, NATIONAL IDENTITIES AND THE USA WORLD CUP

Edited by JOHN SUGDEN & ALAN TOMLINSON

POPULAR CULTURAL STUDIES: 4

Hosts and Champions takes a dispassionate look at one of the world's biggest sporting events. Along with the Olympic Games, the soccer World Cup dominates the global sporting calendar of competing nations and of spectators.

It gives the background to soccer's worldwide popularity and looks at where the World Cup has been played and how it has been won.

Including case-study chapters on: Argentina - Brazil - England - Germany - Ireland - Italy - Japan - Norway - Russia - Sweden - USA; and general essays on the growth of the world game, the cultural meanings of soccer and the ever-increasing role of the media in staging the sports spectacle.

The book captures the international impact of soccer and also probes the cultural distinctiveness of the game in the stories of its growth in different countries and nations.

Dr John Sugden is Senior Lecturer in the Division of Sport and Leisure Studies at the University of Ulster, Jordanstown, Northern Ireland. **Dr Alan Tomlinson** is Professor of Leisure Studies in the Chelsea School, University of Brighton, England.

1994   336 pages   Hbk   1 85742 227 9   £35.00
Pbk   1 85742 228 7   £14.95

Price subject to change without notification

arena

GAME WITHOUT FRONTIERS

FOOTBALL, IDENTITY AND MODERNITY

Edited by **RICHARD GIULIANOTTI & JOHN WILLIAMS**

POPULAR CULTURAL STUDIES: 5

The 1994 World Cup Finals in the United States have again demonstrated the conflicts which exist around football over its international future. The multi-media age beckons new audiences for top-level matches, but worries remain that the historical and cultural appeal of football itself may be the real loser. The 'global game' has a breadth of skills, playing techniques, supporting styles and ruling bodies. These are all subject to local and national traditions of team play and fan display. Modern commercial influences and international cultural links through players and fan styles, are accommodated within the game to an increasing extent. Yet, football's ability to differentiate remains: at local, regional, national and even continental levels.

Essays by leading academics and researchers draw on inter-disciplinary researches in England, Scotland, France, Italy, Germany, Austria, Argentina and Australia.

Richard Giulianotti is currently employed by Aberdeen University's Sociology Department as ESRC Research Assistant on a research project studying Scottish football fan behaviour and related youth sub-cultures. **John Williams** is Senior Researcher at the Sir Norman Chester Centre for Football Research at Leicester University.

1994   356 pages   Hbk   1 85742 219 8   £35.00
Pbk   1 85742 220 1   £14.95

Price subject to change without notification

arena

THE MARGINS OF THE CITY

GAY MEN'S URBAN LIVES

Edited by **STEPHEN WHITTLE**

POPULAR CULTURAL STUDIES: 6

Within cities, gay life has always been marginalised. Despite the fact that their significant places are often centrally placed geographically within cities, gay communities are not centrally placed in the political, social and cultural lives of cities. These international accounts draw on first hand ethnographic research and reflect the responses of gay men in particular to the changes that have taken place during the last 25 years in urban settings. They look at the physical and spatial development of gay places, at the same time as viewing the social placing of the communities that use those places.

The cross-disciplinary studies within this book look at the tensions that arise between gay communities and their cities, the political and economic implications to city planners of the "pink pound" and the legal and social implications for gay men as they attempt to reconcile being both the outsiders and insiders of city life.

Stephen Whittle is Lecturer in Law at Manchester Metropolitan University.

1994   184 pages   Hbk   1 85742 201 5   £29.95
Pbk   1 85742 202 3   £12.95

Price subject to change without notification

THE GULF WAR DID NOT HAPPEN

POLITICS, CULTURE, AND WARFARE POST-VIETNAM

Edited by JEFFREY WALSH

POPULAR CULTURAL STUDIES: 7

This interdisciplinary collection of essays breaks new ground in studying the complex relationships between the historical Gulf war of 1990–91, and those myths, narratives and extended images commonly drawn upon to explain it. Such a distinctive mode of enquiry reveals the ideological symmetry between the political debate and popular culture, or between foreign policy and artistic production. A linking theme running through the volume is the shadow of Vietnam, how the Gulf war was perhaps the culminating event in what has come to be known as "the Vietnam syndrome".

As well as focusing upon the central role of mass media the contributors address issues and events that are not usually treated in the same political and historical context, for example, popular music, comic books, war memorials, anti-war expression, literature, and the effects of war upon language. These essays will be of great interest for students of history, politics, war studies, American studies, cultural studies, oriental and Middle Eastern studies, the social sciences, media studies, literature and art history.

Jeffrey Walsh is Principal Lecturer in English at Manchester Metropolitan University.

1995   224 pages   Hbk   1 85742 292 9   £35.00
Pbk   1 85742 286 4   £12.95

Price subject to change without notification